AT THE SCENT OF WATER

At the Scent of Water

The Ground of Hope
in the Book of Job

J. Gerald Janzen

WILLIAM B. EERDMANS PUBLISHING COMPANY

GRAND RAPIDS, MICHIGAN / CAMBRIDGE, U.K.

Published 2009 by
Wm. B. Eerdmans Publishing Co.
2140 Oak Industrial Drive N.E., Grand Rapids, Michigan 49505 /
P.O. Box 163, Cambridge CB3 9PU U.K.

Printed in the United States of America

15 14 13 12 11 10 09   7 6 5 4 3 2 1

ISBN 978-0-8028-4829-1

www.eerdmans.com

For Holly
Daniel and Amy
Bobby and Lucy

Contents

Foreword, by Patrick D. Miller   ix

Preface   xiii

1. "Extremes Too Hard to Comprehend at Once"   1

2. Israel's Default Position before God   15

3. Tracing the Pattern Elsewhere in the Bible   38

4. Trying to Grasp with Hand and Mind   47

5. Lust for Life and the Bitterness of Job   68

6. Job's Oath   87

7. God's Response, Job's Response, and Final Resolution   95

8. Further on Job and Naomi   111

A Personal Epilogue in Three Parts   117

Acknowledgments   136

Foreword

Few books of Scripture command as intense an interest and fascination as does the book of Job. While exegetes have puzzled and argued over its meaning, the issues it poses and the literary skill in which they are presented have also caught the attention of musicians, artists, dramatists, and poets. Its appeal is manifold, evident in its literary form, its soaring rhetoric, and its poetic beauty. Yet when push comes to shove, Job's attraction rests finally on its insistent and uncompromising attempt to speak to the most fundamental issues of human life: goodness, justice, human suffering, and the reality of God. It is not surprising that one hears the question, What is a human being? (Job 7:1), alongside the question, What is the Almighty? (Job 21:15). The inseparability of the two is nowhere more evident than in Job, nor is either question more seriously and profoundly engaged than in his story.

The book you are about to read makes no pretense of dealing with all the issues that arise in Job's story or with the many interpretive perspectives proposed for dealing with them. It does, however, offer a profound address of the issues and does not hold back from making large claims about what is at stake and how the book of Job responds to the basic questions of our life before God.

In 1982, Gerald Janzen, one of America's leading biblical scholars, produced a commentary on Job that has come to be one of the most widely read and consulted treatments of the book. One would think a major commentary would represent his last word on the subject. Such is not the case with Janzen, as those who know him well will recognize. Again and again, he will produce a fresh and convincing interpretation of a text, a word, or a book and then go back and uncover new meaning and insight into the passage already dealt with. Editors planning to publish an essay or book of his have to be alerted that, before it is published, Janzen may come forth with further material shedding new light on the matter.

So it is with this study of Job, the difference being that more than twenty-five years have elapsed since his commentary. That large part of his lifetime is one of the lenses through which Janzen interprets Job. His personal experiences and relationships play a significant role in his comment. One should not assume, however, that the aim of the author is to talk about himself. The personal references are part of his hermeneutic. Contemporary interpretation pays much attention to context. Janzen, however, is not interested in identifying his social setting or personal views as a context for reading Job. Rather, he brings to the table insight from whatever source helps to understand what Job is about. One may figure out that Eileen is Gerry's wife and Holly and Daniel his children, but when they are spotted in this reading it is not so much to tell his story as it is because his deep store of memories — he never forgets a thing — is like a computer, a personal Wikipedia, that can be Googled again and again to draw out a moment, a memory that illumines what he is saying about the text.

The personal dimension comes to the fore especially in the Epilogue, and here Janzen is self-consciously autobiographical. He recounts three experiences, two of them having to do with his own struggles — and they are as much with preaching as they are about his bout with cancer — and how the book of Job was present, not so much to illumine all that was going on or to answer the big questions implicit in the experience as to provide texts on which to hold, words that carried him on the journey and in their own way were sufficient, providing enough light to see in the darkness. The third part of the personal epilogue is wonderfully titled "Job and My Parents." Here Janzen goes back in time, via the discovery of a now ages-old correspondence between his parents, to find a Joban connection between himself and his father and to search for how it was that his parents found in their relationship and their life together "the gracious, kindly, and unobtrusive presence and grace" of God.

The reader should not skip over the title — or two titles — of the book. They are, as they should be, important indicators of what the book is about. "At the scent of water," a phrase from Job 14, is a pointer to how much the natural world, God's creation, is at the center of the book of Job as Janzen reads it. Most readers of the book of Job may not be aware of how much rain plays a part in its outcome, but they will be when they have finished this book. The lead title, drawn from the poetry and imagery of Job, is given a theological character in the subtitle. While there have been many different ways to characterize the book of Job or to say what it is about, rarely will one find it presented as a book about hope. Yet that is precisely Janzen's primary claim. His hermeneutic is one of retrieval and trust. I expect many readers will find that surprising, but also persuasive.

Other dimensions of this book belong to its hermeneutic. One is Janzen's wonderful ability to tease out of particular words in the Hebrew text profound and crucial clues to what the text is about. Attention to vocabulary is an automatic part of good exegesis. No one practices that better than Janzen. Nor is his approach a matter of dry word study. It is more like an animal sniffing around in the debris of the forest expecting to find something good to eat but not knowing for sure that will happen until it has probed here and there, checking this spot and that root (pun intended). While Janzen collects data in the process, that is not his goal. It is seeing and making connections that are sensible and persuasive, such that the reader will say, "Yes, I see that."

If Janzen can and does read deeply into the language of the text, he is not dependent upon that alone. He draws on spheres of literature and knowledge not customarily a part of biblical interpretation. Anyone who knows him is aware of the reservoir of poetry nestled within his mind. No conversation goes on for long without his tapping into that store and quoting lines of poetry that come to his mind in regard to the subject under discussion. It is not always immediately clear to the conversation partner why and how the quoted lines connect to the subject of conversation. What one learns to do is wait a bit and keep listening. The connection may be developed slowly, perhaps circular in character, or moving out in one direction and then cutting back in another. Eventually, the listener/reader will see — to one's joy and delight — how the poetry has caught and illumined what it is that Janzen is thinking or talking about. While he is widely versed in poetry of all sorts, one or two poets in particular seem often to provide the way of speaking about the issue of the text that Janzen wishes to expose to the light. In this case, as often, it is Robert Frost. One may rightly identify Frost as Janzen's favorite poet, except that the point is not "Who is your favorite poet?" It is rather whose poetic way of seeing and speaking about the world is most helpful in seeing truth and meaning, in the text and in our life.

We are in an era when various nonbiblical and nontheological fields of knowledge are believed to provide resources for understanding the Bible, especially literary theory, sociology, social history and criticism, and politics. Janzen has always moved in a different direction, finding guidance in both philosophy, especially Whitehead, and psychology. The latter gets little attention in biblical studies, aside from references here and there to D. W. Winnicott and a few others. For a long time Janzen has found the neglect of psychology and what we can learn from it a puzzling aspect of biblical studies. Here as elsewhere he has moved to overcome the lapse, drawing upon developmental psychology, and especially the work of Erik Erikson, W. W. Meissner, and Daniel Stern, to uncover in human development a reflection of what Janzen sees as the fundamental movement between two biblical paradigms: "the relation between Abrahamic and Mosaic religion as models of the divine-human relation" (p. 15). Much of the first half of the book is devoted to explaining these models and how they are related to each other. It is not until the end of Chapter Three that the reader finally gets to Job. It would be a large mistake, however, to jump to that part of the book and skip the first three chapters, for this opening discussion is the key to understanding the book as Janzen interprets it. What's more, as he himself recognizes, what he has set forth in these three chapters is a miniature Old Testament theology, powerful and persuasive. Even as one reads Janzen's discussion of these paradigms with Job in view, one realizes that here is a construct against which Scripture as a whole should be read. The result is a deeper and clearer understanding of Job but also a resource for thinking afresh about all sorts of texts, problematic and otherwise. That is a lot to take away from a book on Job.

PATRICK D. MILLER

Preface

In 1985 John Knox Press published my commentary on the book of Job, in its series *Interpretation: Commentary for Preachers and Teachers*. In that commentary I attempted to interpret this biblical book, chapter by chapter, as I had come to understand it in the course of studying it in the company of students over a period of twenty years. In the present book, the result of another twenty years of wrestling with this dark angel, I take a different approach. Rather than a chapter-by-chapter commentary, I have taken a thematic approach in which, through an exploration of key images and basic frameworks of understanding in Job and the Bible generally, I attempt to lay out the essential issues at the heart of Job's agony and the debates with his friends.

I make no pretense to have done justice to this Mount Everest of a biblical book. I suspect that, unlike Everest, its summit will remain forever unscaled by mere commentators. But, like Mallory, the British mountaineer who, when asked why he climbed high mountains, is reported to have said, "because they are there," and whose frozen body was found on the mountainside, decades after he was last seen within a few hundred yards of the peak before the mists closed in around him, I would be content to be thought of as one found somewhere on this book's upper slopes. The present book is offered as one man's map of the terrain as he has traversed it.

1. "Extremes Too Hard to Comprehend at Once"

The book of Job opens with the words "There was a man in the land of Uz whose name was Job." Wherever Uz is, it is not Israel but another country. And Job appears to be an ancient name, suggesting, as one scholar says, "a hero of great antiquity." The effect of such an opening is to place Job at a distance from the reader, like stories that begin "Once upon a time" or "Long ago and far away." In the case of fables and fairy stories, such an opening allows us to enjoy the tale that is about to unfold without raising questions about the credibility of things that happen within it, such as animals that speak or humans with extraordinary powers. For the world we enter when we begin to read is not our own world of here-and-now. It is not governed by the laws nor limited by the possibilities that circumscribe our lives. In the "time and place" — in the imaginative world — of this story we may fly through the air with the hero in blithe indifference to the pull of gravity. Of course, when we return to our own world we land with a thump that speaks all too clearly of the gravity of our time and place.

The words that open the book of Job, in distancing the action from us, serve a different purpose. The tale they introduce is all too familiar to us, unfolding within a world very much like our own, a world in which grave calamities can befall us without warning or apparent reason or purpose. Such calamities can be so painful in their raw immediacy as to be unbearable. We must hold them at a distance. So we hit the "mute" button in our brain to render the unbearable details indistinct and to quiet, for now, the questions they raise.

When those questions become insistent enough, we often find ourselves responding indirectly. One psychologist has proposed that Stephen

King's horror stories are, in part, a way of coping with a terrible tragedy in his childhood in which he escaped unscathed but a buddy was killed. C. S. Lewis, who had written and lectured on the problem of evil, was shattered by the death of his wife, Joy. He responded in part by keeping a diary that he subsequently published under the title *A Grief Observed*. In attempting to come to terms with his loss, it is as though Lewis found it important, not simply to experience that grief, but to achieve a certain distance from it in observing it. "I . . . live each endless day in grief," he wrote. "But what am I to do? I must have some drug, and reading isn't a strong enough drug now. By writing it all down . . . I believe I get a little outside it."[1] If writing the diary helped him get a little outside of his grief, in publishing it he presumably hoped that others, in reading it, might likewise get a little outside of their own grief, by observing their grief indirectly through his.

If, then, the book of Job was written during or shortly after Israel's defeat, Jerusalem's destruction and the exile of its leading citizens at the hands of the Babylonians, we may view it as the attempt of one survivor to engage the suffering and the questions that arose out of that calamity, and to do so indirectly by telling the story of a man named Job who lived long ago and far away. Likewise, in reading about Job and his friends we too may be enabled to get a little outside the griefs that we have undergone and to engage indirectly the questions that they have left us with. How did they attempt to cope with what Shakespeare's Hamlet called "The heart-ache and the thousand natural shocks/That flesh is heir to"?

Hand and Mind — and Heart, If Need Be

I have found it helpful, in recent years, to cope with Joban suffering and the questions it raises with the help of a short poem by Robert Frost, "The Armful."[2] As is so often the case with Frost's poetry, this poem opens on an everyday scene that before long takes on a great freight of meaning.

> For every parcel I stoop down to seize,
> I lose some other off my arms and knees,
> And the whole pile is slipping, bottles, buns,

1. C. S. Lewis, *A Grief Observed* (New York: Seabury, 1961) 12.
2. *Collected Poems, Prose, & Plays* (New York: Library of America, 1995) 245.

Extremes too hard to comprehend at once,
Yet nothing I should care to leave behind.
With all I have to hold with, hand and mind
And heart, if need be, I will do my best
To keep their building balanced at my breast.
I crouch down to prevent them as they fall;
Then sit down in the middle of them all.
I had to drop the armful in the road
And try to stack them in a better load.

The scene is a homely one, familiar to anyone homebound with an armful of groceries. How is one to hold on to several bags of groceries at once? What adds to the difficulty is that the bags contain "extremes too hard to comprehend at once" — round hard bottles and soft squishy buns. Bottles alone could be held tightly. Buns must be carried gently so as not to flatten them. But how can a person carry both at one and the same time? Clasp the packages tightly and the buns — not to mention the ripe bananas — will be flattened. Carry them loosely and the heavy bottles may slip and break through the bag or spill out of it. We read the opening lines with a rueful smile of recognition.

But Frost soon tips us off that in this poem he is really wrestling with another kind of load, for we do not usually speak of "comprehending" an armful of groceries. The word comes from the Latin verb *prehendere,* "to grasp, seize," a verb that underlies our word "prehensile" as in our phrase, "prehensile thumb" — a thumb that, as my *Webster's* says, is "adapted for seizing or grasping, esp. by wrapping around." While our related word "apprehend" can refer to acts of physical or mental grasping (a cop may apprehend a criminal; a forecast of severe weather may fill us with apprehension), we usually think of comprehension as "wrapping our mind around" something so as to understand it.

Hand and Mind

As Frost sees it, we grasp and comprehend things in three different ways: with our hand, with our mind, and with our heart. The first is the soonest learned, for who has not felt or observed an infant of a few days instinctively grasping the finger gently placed into its tiny palm? With the passing

3

weeks and months, the hand becomes an organ of increasingly wide-ranging exploration, grasping objects left and right, soft and hard, and drawing them to the infant's mouth to see what they feel and taste like in that organ of its young appetite for life. Throughout our lives the hand remains the primary tool, and a primary symbol, of our ability to explore, understand, and manipulate our world. When I was a child and something went wrong with one of my toys or little construction projects, an older brother would often say, "Here, let me fix it for you," or "Can I give you a hand?" And I would look on in admiration while those older, more capable hands would work the fix or show me how to make something. Contemporary technology simply extends this ability in marvelous ways and in many different directions, from infinitesimally small computer chips to gigantic earth-moving machines, and from space-exploring rocketry to tiny gizmos that promise to travel around in our bloodstream and monitor the microbiological processes that go on there. But even in this way of comprehending, we need to learn how to hold things of different qualities. We hold radioisotopes indirectly, by means of long metallic robotic arms and hands; but we hold a baby gently in our own hands. We carry a load of bricks firmly; but baby and bricks may be extremes too hard to hold at once, and it may be wiser to attend first to one and then to the other.

Some things elude our physical ability to grasp or fix manually. This may be because we as individuals may not have the "hands-on" ability. But we can still try to understand through observation and reflection and to share that understanding with others. As a teacher I used to wince at the jibe "them as can, does; them as can't, teach." But the world of sports is full of coaches who were average or even mediocre athletes but whose powers of observation, imaginative reflection, and communicative skill have made them superb teachers. (Butch Harmon could never win a golfing major, but he coached Tiger Woods, who has won several.) And the world of sports also provides examples of superb athletes who made poor coaches. The ability to comprehend with our minds and the ability to comprehend with our hands are close cousins. Each makes its own distinctive contribution to our well-being, and each offers its own peculiar pleasures. I watch with envious admiration while the man at the griddle behind the counter with practiced ease turns my "once over easy" egg and serves it up perfectly on the plate. Then I turn to the *New York Times* crossword puzzle and work at it until, with a feeling of satisfaction, I solve the last remaining mystery.

4

The satisfaction we derive from solving crosswords or other puzzle games is a trivial example of a drive that marks us as human beings: the drive to understand, even where understanding has no immediate practical utility. It seems that this drive is built into us. It is as though we were designed for understanding, and arriving at understanding brings with it a sense of the rightness of things, a rightness in which this incessant drive can for a moment find rest. I remember spending an early morning hour with a nephew who was having difficulty with his sums. He couldn't seem to grasp why, in adding columns of numbers where each row had two or more digits, you start from the right and carry to the left. Why not start from the left? And what was this "carrying" business? His teacher had said only, "That's just how it's done." His insistent "why?" prevented him from grasping the technique, and he was almost in tears. After a moment, I hit on a way of breaking the problem down to its component parts, so that he could see why it had to be done that way. Then I set him several sums, and he added them up swiftly and correctly. When he had finished, he put his pencil down, rested his cheeks in the palms of his hands, stared at the page for a moment, and then said in a low, almost purring voice, "Math is cool!"

It is always cool to understand "why." Or the peace of mind may have a different quality, such as consolation. When someone dies inexplicably, an autopsy will not bring them back to life; but its results can give some ease of mind to the survivors. When someone is murdered, the concern is not only to apprehend the murderer, but to learn, if possible, why the deed was done. To discover that someone has killed someone else "just for the hell of it" (one thinks of the schoolboys in Vermont who killed two college professors just because they wanted to kill someone) is to add a dimension of profound absurdity to a calamity already grievous enough. Such an act just doesn't make sense.

In grasping things with our hands, we learn to grasp them differently depending on whether they are hard or soft — bottles or buns, bricks or babies. What of the things we grasp with our minds? Are some matters best comprehended firmly and others gently? Are some questions best approached directly and literally — "head-on," so to speak — while others are best approached indirectly, tangentially, figuratively, metaphorically?

The realm of logic received classic definition in Aristotle's distinction between identity and difference: A is A; A is not B. A thing is what it is and not something else. Apples are not oranges. This logic is the basis of the binary computer whose two symbols are 1 and 0. All computer functions, no matter how complex, finally come down to variable patterns of ones and zeroes.

But while this logic — this way of grasping things firmly, directly, and literally — is fundamental to one way of acting and of knowing, it is not the only way. Poetry, while it can use this "A is A" logic (as in Gertrude Stein's celebrated, "A rose is a rose is a rose"), also flagrantly employs a logic in which A is B, as where we might say, "My love is a red, red rose." When e. e. cummings ends a sonnet to his lady love with the words "lady through whose profound and fragile lips/the sweet small clumsy feet of April came/into the ragged meadow of my soul,"[3] do these words say something that could be stated more directly, more accurately, through the logic of "A is A; A is not B"? Or are the figures of speech and his poetic indirection the most precise, most adequate means available to him for saying what wants to be said — for comprehending, insofar as it can be comprehended — what wants to be comprehended?

But this leads to our third way of comprehending: with our heart. It is part of the essential and enduring delight of love, that it remains unfathomable by merely intellectual comprehension and unexhausted by ever so many words and acts. "How do I love thee? Let me count the ways," says Elizabeth Barrett Browning.[4] And when she has finished her sonnet, she has hardly begun to canvass the possibilities. Even the indirections of poetry only convey inklings of *what it is* that we hold in our hearts. And as to *why* we love someone, answers of the sort that attempt to explain love in terms of its value for adaptation in the evolutionary scramble for survival miss the point; they end up talking about something other than the subject of Browning's poem. The only finally adequate answer is that we love someone because they are who they are and we are who we are, and a lifetime is not long enough to enter into the mystery of who they are and of who we might become in light of who they are. It is a mystery that can be held only in the heart — a heart that finds itself called on to grow along with the growing mystery it harbors.

---

3. e. e. cummings, "if I have made, my lady, intricate," *Poems, 1923-1954* (New York: Harcourt, Brace & World, 1968) 219.

4. Elizabeth Barrett Browning, "How Do I Love Thee?" (Montreal: Pocket Books of Canada, 1944) 177.

. . . and Heart, If Need Be

The irony is that some of the things that can be held only with the heart we would rather hold with anything but the heart. That is why Frost says, "and heart, if need be." When things go wrong our first impulse is to want to fix them — and if we can't fix them at least to explain them, make sense of them. If we can't fix them or make sense of them — if their absurdity threatens to render life itself absurd — the temptation is to re-describe them, re-define them, turn them into events or situations that will fit into our systems of understanding. But in doing so, we do not explain them; we explain them away. Or, if we do not deal with them in this way, we may suppress them, and even repress them. In his biography of Bishop John A. T. Robinson, Eric James writes that "John was a man of deep feeling but emotions that did not respond to reason were neither admitted in himself nor easily understood in others."[5] Later, James reports an exchange between Robinson and his son. The son asked him, "What do you do with feelings you don't know what to do with?"[6] The father responded, "I don't have them." In the same vein, James reports the comment of a daughter: "One of the unwritten rules was that you don't get upset; or if you do, you find the quickest, most logical way of altering circumstances so that there's nothing to be upset about. . . . I learnt how to side-step feelings so that they glanced off me, barely acknowledged."[7]

The preceding quotations are not meant to hold a man up to disapprobation. Far from it. As a "scholar, pastor, prophet" (the subtitle of the biography), Robinson made a huge difference for good in many lives, in his capacity both to bring intellectual comprehension to the study of the Scriptures and of contemporary life and to effect significant change in the lives of people within his pastoral care and through his prophetic utterances on the contemporary scene. His sermon at the funeral of a sixteen-year-old girl who had died of cancer was treasured by the mother, who included it in the book she later wrote about her daughter. What these quotations do bring home with great poignancy is that there are things that lie at the very center of our lives which cannot be comprehended with our hand or our mind, and that these include aspects of our lives — aspects of the actual

5. Eric James, *A Life of Bishop John A. T. Robinson* (Grand Rapids: Wm. B. Eerdmans, 1988) 32.

6. James, *A Life of Bishop John A. T. Robinson,* 169.

7. James, *A Life of Bishop John A. T. Robinson,* 170.

world — that we would give anything not to have to hold with our heart. Robert Frost's sister Jeannie spent a good deal of her life in a mental hospital in Maine. He once observed that she never forgave him for not going crazy with her over the badness of the world. One suspects that his poetry, in all its figural indirection, was his way of sitting down, again and again, in the middle of his life and trying to stack in a better load the extremes that he so often found too hard to comprehend at once.

Extremes

It would be a revealing exercise to ask the members of a group to take a sheet of paper and, in light of Frost's poem, to make a list of those "extremes" they find too hard to comprehend at once in their own lives or in society, and then to compare notes and discuss them. Here are two topics on my own list: (1) Individual liberty and communal responsibility; or, in different terms, rights and obligations. How do I "balance at my breast" the often-felt opposing pulls of those claims that I feel I may rightfully make on others and those claims that others make on me? How do I decide when I may best serve others by setting my claims aside to respond to theirs and when I may best serve others by voicing my claims and holding others accountable to them? (2) The vast disparity in scale between myself as a finite individual and the ever-expanding universe. In the year after my graduation from high school, this "extreme" literally overwhelmed me and plunged me into a life-crisis of shattering intensity. How do I take my own life seriously — how do I take anyone's life seriously — or even the life of the human race taken as a whole — when I consider how infinitesimally small human life is within that unfathomable cosmic ocean, that vast cosmic desert? As Bishop Bossuet put it in the seventeenth century, in a sermon on death,

> if I look backward, what an infinite expanse of time in which I do not exist! And if I look forward, what a dreadful continuation in which I no longer exist! And that I shall occupy so small a space in this immense abysm of time! I am nothing — an interval so small is not capable of distinguishing me from nothingness.[8]

8. Quoted in Thomas McFarland, *Coleridge and the Pantheist Tradition* (Oxford: Clarendon, 1969) 125 (my translation).

Even in this short interval, space stretches out from me, from us all, unfathomably in all directions. Who then, what then, are we? Is this what Job felt after God's first address to him? In 40:4 he says, "I am of small account." The Hebrew text says simply *qalloti,* "I am small" — or as we might say, "I feel *so small!*" The awareness is both palpably physical and painfully existential. The vastness of the scene that God paints for him in the first address leaves him feeling like a speck of dust before the creation's overwhelming grandeur, and more so before the awesome mystery of its Creator. It leaves him also with a sense of his own utter insignificance, like the ash heap he is sitting on. But he had already said, in 30:19, "He has cast me into the mire, and I have become like dust and ashes." Does God in the first address simply underline and reinforce that conclusion? We shall see.

Another pair of extremes that crops up again and again in theological writing and religious conversation is the tension between justice and mercy, or between justice and compassion — between "hard" and "soft" virtues. A closely related pair of extremes — or perhaps the same pair in different terms — is the tension between law and grace. When is the letter of the law to be followed and, if necessary, enforced with penalties; and when, left to its own logic, does it become so hard and harsh as to be inhumane and beg to be seasoned with mercy? When does mercy become sentimental indulgence, devoid of any backbone, spoiling and corrupting its objects, and crying out for accountability? How do we, at one and the same time, follow the injunction "to do justly, and to love mercy" (Mic 6:8 KJV)? How does God, at one and the same time, answer the psalmist's prayer for mercy and justice (Ps 119:156) or betroth Israel to himself "in righteousness and in justice, in steadfast love, and in mercy" (Hos 2:19)?

Another pair of extremes poses even graver difficulties, extremes that go by a variety of names: anticipation and apprehension; hope and despair; an appetite for life and bitterness over what life can throw in our teeth; a sense of life's worthwhileness and a sense of the futility of all things. How do we sustain an appetite for life; how do we get up in the morning willing to meet the new day, in the face of the kind of suffering, tragedy, and evil that past days have witnessed and that the coming day may hold in store? Like many other Canadians, I grew up on a skating rink. As a parent in Indianapolis I became concerned that my children would grow up culturally deprived and alienated from their Canadian ancestry unless they were given an opportunity to taste the sense of freedom and grace that skating makes possible. So I took them to a local covered rink, rented skates for the three of us, and led them out on to the ice. They moved tentatively and awkwardly at first, then gradually glided with the beginnings of rhythm. Suddenly, Daniel's feet went out from under him and he landed on his back, his head hitting the ice with a resounding crack. After a few moments of solicitous comfort from his sister Holly, I proposed that we resume our progress around the rink; but he said, "No thanks, Dad — I've lost my will to skate." How do we recover our will to skate, when life knocks our feet out from under us?

In a group exercise such as I have imagined, the combined list of extremes would no doubt be extensive. If we were asked to rank them in order of difficulty of comprehension, I would without hesitation lift up these two pairs: our own smallness, and the threat of our own insignificance, as measured against the immensity of the space-time universe; and an appetite for life over against the suffering, tragedy, and evil whose eruptions threaten to embitter and quench it.

Touching What Cannot Be Grasped

In Robert Browning's poem "Andrea del Sarto," the title character says, "a man's reach should exceed his grasp,/Or what's a heaven for?"[9] The man is a painter; and one suspects that Browning has him allude to that part of the fresco on the ceiling of the Sistine Chapel in Rome where Michaelangelo has painted Adam with arm outstretched heavenward and God with arm outstretched earthward, their index fingers almost touching. Our reach should exceed our grasp. Certainly, it does. Anyone who has tried to reach something on a high shelf, or to change a light bulb in a high-ceilinged room, knows how frustrating it is to be able to touch an object with the tip of a finger but not to grasp it; for the attempt to grasp it involves a curling of the fingers and thereby a shortening of one's reach. But if our reach *does* exceed our grasp, why *should* it?

The poem makes clear that at one time del Sarto aspired to great things artistically. But as time went on he settled for something less. He settled for what he knew he could paint, for what lay well within his grasp. In Frost's words, he "left behind" that earlier aspiration. Better to succeed

9. *The Complete Poetical Works of Robert Browning* (New York: Macmillan, 1925) 452.

at what he knew he could do than fail in the attempt to reach his earlier vision. Besides, it paid the rent. But when we settle for living only in relation to what we can grasp and hold, understand and use — only for what will pay the rent — we lose something vital.

Frost's poem poses the question of what to do with those issues in life that we cannot get either our hands or our minds around. Do we learn to "not have" them? Do we, for example, define reality as what we can show to be true — what we can grasp — through the actions and theories of the scientific method or the operations of mathematical logic? Or do we acknowledge that there are realities that we encounter and undergo only in touching them, and that we may "hold" them only in keeping them balanced at our breast? And are the extremes of justice and mercy, law and grace, suffering and hope, and finally, our place among the immensities of the cosmos, among those realities?

One of the psalms provides us with an image that I have come to see as going to the heart of these questions. I shall return to it in a later chapter, but it will be helpful to consider it here briefly, as a way of drawing this chapter to a conclusion. It is Psalm 131.

> [1] O Lord, my heart is not lifted up,
>   my eyes are not raised too high;
>   I do not occupy myself with things
>   too great and too marvelous for me.
> [2] But I have calmed and quieted my soul,
>   like a weaned child with its mother;
>   my soul is like the weaned child that is with me.
> [3] O Israel, hope in the Lord
>   from this time on and forevermore.

Two comments on the translation. First, the Hebrew word translated "marvelous" in some contexts (for example, 2 Samuel 13:2) refers to an action deemed "difficult," or "impossible." Where translated as "marvelous" or "wonderful," it refers to divine wonders that exceed the capacity of humans to understand or fathom. Second, the preposition twice translated "with" in verse 2 has, in its most basic and literal usage, the meaning "on, upon." For example, in Isa 66:12 it occurs twice in the lines, "you shall nurse and be carried *on* her arm,/and dandled *on* her knees." Patrick D. Miller, along with other recent scholars, translates Ps 131:2 this way: "Like a weaned child *on* its mother,/Like the weaned child *on* me is my soul."[10]

The voice we hear in this psalm is apparently the voice of a woman, a mother, who is distressed and agitated over some issue in her life or in her world that is "too great and too difficult" for her to do anything about or to grasp with her understanding. The whole matter is, as we say, beyond her. It is beyond her grasp. Yet it is not completely beyond her. She can touch it, for it is touching her and troubling her deeply.

In the midst of her own agitation and distress, this woman finds her young child coming to her in a similar state, upset over something or other in its own little world. At an earlier stage she would have taken it up and comforted it by nursing it at her breast, like the scene in Isa 66:10-13. But the child is too old for this, for it is a weaned child. As it curls up on her lap, she observes how the child calms and quiets itself. It is as though, having (as psychologists would say) internalized its mother's earlier acts of comfort at the breast, the child soothes itself, saying to itself, "There, there, it's all right. You are safe and secure with your mother, and she will see to things." Seeing the child calm and quiet itself on her lap, she finds herself doing likewise, curling up, as it were, on the lap of the God who has given her life and who, she trusts, will "see to things" that are too great and too difficult for her. In doing so, she may be said to embody and exemplify the response that God elicits from Israel during the exile (Isa 46:3-4).

> [3] Hearken to me, O house of Jacob,
>   all the remnant of the house of Israel,
>   who have been borne by me from your birth,
>   carried from the womb;
> [4] even to your old age I am He,
>   and to gray hairs I will carry you.
>   I have made, and I will bear;
>   I will carry and will save.

The capacity to bear what is unbearable rests in the awareness that one is being borne up in the midst of what is too difficult to change, to understand, perhaps even to feel. And where even this awareness does not enable us to

---

10. Patrick D. Miller, *They Cried to the Lord: The Form and Theology of Biblical Prayer* (Minneapolis: Fortress, 1994) 239 (italics added).

hold everything together, what such images encourage us to do is to drop everything, not simply "in the middle of the road," but into the lap of God.

Note to the Reader

The following two chapters are not about the book of Job, except at the very end of Chapter Three. They are important, however, as offering a biblical background against which Job's story plays out. They have to do with the formation of the "mind-set" within which Job and his friends wrestle so agonizingly over his calamities, and with the question of whether that mind-set itself contributes to his agonies and to the futility of the friends' attempts to help him. These chapters also concern the possibility that Job's recovery from his calamities involves coming to a different mind-set, or rather, recovering a deeper, more adequate mind-set, which will enable him, if not to understand his experiences with his mind, to bear them in his heart.

Job's calamities throw him into a "crisis of faith." They call into question his deepest beliefs and understandings — beliefs and understandings that he inherits from generations of the teaching and experience of his ancestors. His crisis threatens to destroy those beliefs, and to leave those understandings lying about him like the rubble left after a military assault on a walled city, or like the chaos left by a tsunami or hurricane. The question is whether he can any longer believe what his ancestors believed and what he himself had believed before his calamities. The book of Job poses the same question to those readers whose fundamental religious beliefs have been grounded in and shaped by the biblical story. But before those readers conclude that Job's calamities, or their own, render them unable to believe any longer the Bible's "old, old story," it is worth taking the time to reconsider what the biblical story is. Put in this way, the question is not only whether the biblical story about God can survive the crisis of Job, but also whether that story has been adequately understood. In the next two chapters, I offer my version of a miniature "Old Testament Theology in Outline" as a basis for interpreting the book of Job. I offer it also as a means by which we may assess whether Job's story renders the biblical story unbelievable or whether it calls for us to revise our way of reading it.

I shall give a brief summary of the following two chapters at the beginning of Chapter Four. It may be helpful to read that summary at this point, and then return to these two chapters. By getting them under our belt, so to speak, we will be more fully equipped to recognize what deep issues underlie Job's agonized questions and the friends' attempts to help him, and also to appreciate how God's addresses to Job finally enable him, not only to live with what has happened to him, but to go on with a life that had threatened to end in bitter disillusion and despair.

2. Israel's Default Position before God

In Chapter One I proposed that, by introducing Job as a person who had lived "long ago and far away," the writer was offering an opportunity for the readers and hearers of this book to engage their own sufferings indirectly. But even when stories take us for a time out of our own situation, we still in some sense read them through internal eyeglasses whose lenses have been ground by the experience and understanding of our own society. In growing up within our society, we internalize and "make our own" how our society typically comprehends life issues — how it typically holds them with hand, head, and heart. I have referred to such ways of understanding as "mind-sets." These mind-sets for the most part are operative within us without our thinking about them. They are like the inner workings of our computers, which most of us don't think about while we work on letters or papers or explore the Internet, and which only the technicians and amateur computer geeks bother to think about and work on. Nowadays, those who reflect on "mind-sets," as ways of understanding and living in the world, may call such mind-sets "models" or "paradigms" of reality. As examples in the field of science, we may point to the Ptolemaic understanding of the universe, in which the earth was the center around which all heavenly bodies revolved, and then the Copernican, in which the earth is seen to revolve, with other planets in our system, around the sun. Similarly, we may point to the Newtonian model of the universe and its forces, and then the Einsteinian. In the realm of economics and politics, we may contrast free enterprise capitalism in a democratic context and Marxist communism in a single-party political system. Each provides a model or paradigm, a systematic pattern of relationships, within which more particular concerns and issues are both understood and engaged. To be born and raised in America is, for most of us, to believe instinctively and unreflectively that free-market capitalism is not only the best economic system, but the only system that makes sense, while, say, Marxism is not only inefficient but nonsensical and morally suspect for what it does to individual freeedom and initiative. But if one is born and raised in a Marxist society, it may well mean for such a person that that economic system is the only one that makes sense insofar as the interests and welfare of the community as a whole rightly place limits on individual freedom and initiative. For such a person, democratic capitalism may be viewed as the expression of unbridled individualism devoted to personal advancement to the neglect and at the expense of others less capable. In this chapter, I want to try to sketch in broad strokes two comprehensive ways of understanding life issues — two models or paradigms, producing two kinds of mind-set — that existed among the inheritors of the Israelite tradition at the time when the book of Job was written.

One of these models is associated with Mount Sinai and the figure of Moses. The other model is associated with the figures of Abraham and Sarah and the other ancestors of Israel who appear in Genesis 12–50. In most expositions of the shape of Israel's religion in the Old Testament, Moses and the covenant at Mount Sinai take center stage, while the narratives in Genesis 12–50 are taken as, so to speak, a "warm-up" act that, having done its job, yields the stage for the main, Mosaic act that follows. Consequently, the religion of Israel is understood and expounded primarily in terms of the Mosaic covenant. When, then, the book of Job is read, the questions that trouble Job and his friends — and the questions that trouble the biblically-versed reader — are engaged primarily in terms of that covenant and its logic. In my view, this is to get off on the wrong foot altogether. As I read the Old Testament, fundamental to its proper understanding (and therefore to the understanding of the book of Job) is a right understanding of the relation between Abrahamic and Mosaic religion as models of the divine-human relation. Convinced as I have become of the importance of this issue, it will be necessary in this chapter and the next to spend a good deal of space in exploring these two models and their implications. In doing so, I will employ an analogy drawn from the world of the computer.

Default Positions

Computer lingo has given a new connotation to the old word "default." In my *Webster's New Collegiate Dictionary,*[1] the word was defined as referring primarily to a failure or neglect to perform a duty, pay a financial obligation, appear in court for a scheduled proceeding, or, in sports (where I first heard and used the word), forfeit a match by failure to appear for its start or by failure to complete it.

In computer lingo the word has taken on a different, more positive connotation. According to one edition of *The iMac for Dummies,* in its appendix titled "The Techno-Babble Translation Guide," the word means "the factory settings. For example, the *default* setting for your typing in a word processor is single-spaced, one-inch margins."[2] One can change many of the factory settings for a specific document; but then, when one begins a fresh document (in PC lingo, when one opens a new file), that document will conform to the factory settings. I suppose the word "default" has taken on this meaning because of its use in the earlier phrase "in default of," which means "failing, or in the absence of." When someone refers to "default settings," then, we may take them to mean "in the absence of special *ad hoc* alterations, these are the settings your computer will revert to whenever you open a new file or document."

But it is possible to customize the default settings. If I decide to produce documents with, say, two-inch margins, I pull down the "format" menu on my Mac (PC users will have to translate), select "document," and a dialog box appears in which I can reformat the margins to two inches. In the lower left-hand corner of that box I see a little button labeled "default." If I click on that button, then from now on the default setting for margins is two inches, and not the original factory setting. From now on, whenever I open a new document, I will automatically ("by default") have two-inch margins. If, on opening a new document, I decide to set the margins at one inch, but fail to select default, those one-inch margins will hold good only for that document, and any new document I open will revert to my customized default setting. So we may distinguish three kinds of settings: An *ad hoc* setting, chosen only for the document I am currently working on; a

1. 2nd ed. (Springfield, MA: Merriam, 1960).

2. David Pogue, *The iMac for Dummies* (Foster City, CA: IDG Books Worldwide, 1998) 317.

customized default setting, which will hold good — provide the frame of reference — for every new document I open unless I choose an *ad hoc* setting; and the original default setting which the factory installed.

Why is it important to distinguish between a customized default setting and the original factory setting? From time to time, users will discover that their computer has "crashed." This is a nuisance, but once they are up and running again they will discover, as they open new documents, that their customized default settings are still in force. *However,* a more serious calamity may occur, which the dialog box on the screen identifies (at least, in my Mac) as a "fatal system error." The choice of words here is telling. "Error" normally implies a minor mistake; but "fatal" implies something grave. (There is something worse yet, of course: in my case it was described by the technician as "frying the mother-board," which involved irrecoverable loss of all applications and all documents and necessitated the installation of a new mother-board. When this happened, the screen simply went black and stayed that way.) The fact that the screen can display a dialog box telling me of a fatal system error shows me that the computer is still functional and that the so-called "fatal" error can be rectified. The hard drive is still intact, and rectification involves reinstalling all the software. But since the software disks all come with factory settings, reinstalling the software produces a reversion to original default settings.

Keeping in mind this distinction between original default and customized default settings, let us consider the following questions: (1) What is biblical Israel's default position before God — the enduring frame of reference, the stable foundation, for all the different specific aspects of Israel's relation with God? (2) Is that position its original default position, or is it a customized default position? (3) What happens when a "fatal system error" occurs, such as we see in Exodus 32 with the making of the golden calf, moving God to say to Moses, "your people . . . have corrupted themselves" (32:7)? When that happens, what default system enables the relation between Israel and God to become "up and running" again?

In reflecting on these questions, it will be helpful to make some broad distinctions that mark two periods in Israel's history with God and two segments in the Bible's narrative of that history: (1) The period of Israel's ancestors in Genesis 12–50 beginning with Abraham and Sarah; and (2) the period inaugurated by the covenant-making ceremonies under Moses at Mount Sinai. These two periods, which we may call the Abrahamic and the Mosaic, are marked by two different models or paradigms of divine-human relation. Walter Moberly has sketched these paradigms, in terms of their continuities and their contrasts, in a book entitled *The Old Testament of the Old Testament: Patriarchal Narratives and Mosaic Yahwism.*[3] Before summarizing the distinctions he has drawn, it will be helpful first to place the discussion in its wider ancient Near Eastern context, for Israel did not arise in a vacuum. Its emerging relations with the God whom it came to know as YHWH (or Yahweh; commonly translated "the LORD") show remarkable affinities as well as dramatic contrasts with religious understandings that existed among its Mesopotamian and Canaanite neighbors. In particular, the two paradigms of divine-human relation that we may identify as "Abrahamic" and "Mosaic" in many respects parallel similar paradigms among these ancient neighbors.

Models of Divine-Human Relation in Mesopotamia

In his book, *The Treasures of Darkness: A History of Mesopotamian Religion,* Thorkild Jacobsen analyzes four millennia of Mesopotamian religion in terms of the central metaphor for deity that prevails in a given era.[4] Roughly speaking, he writes, the fourth millennium B.C.E. is marked by the experience of deity as the *élan vital* present in the phenomena of nature — the presence of a mysterious, dynamic activity *within* and *peculiar to* each phenomenon, striving to come to expression *as* that phenomenon. For example, the god Dumuzi is "the élan vital of new life in nature, vegetable and animal, a will and power in it that brings it about."[5] (Think of a baker's yeast which, in rising, seems to have a life of its own.) In the third millennium, which is marked by the rise of city-states, complex economies, stratified administrations, and systems of laws, with kings ruling over all, the gods take on predominantly royal characteristics. No longer vital forces present and active *in* the phenomena of nature and human life, the gods now are experienced and portrayed as transcendent divine figures ruling *over* these phenomena. The human king is the representative on earth of the divine king, the earthly manager of the divine king's realm and estates. Whereas in the earlier time the gods were local, closely connected with the

---

3. (Minneapolis: Fortress, 1992).
4. (New Haven: Yale University Press, 1976).
5. Jacobsen, *The Treasures of Darkness,* 26.

natural phenomena in which they were observed, now the high gods become cosmic in scope. If the religious concerns in the earlier period were primarily economic, now they become (also) prominently political.

The second millennium, says Jacobsen, is marked by the rise of what he calls "personal religion" and what other scholars prefer to call family- or clan-based religion. In this religious paradigm, the deity is conceived in parental terms — the divine father, of whom the male clan leader is the earthly representative; the divine mother, giver of birth. In this setting, the god may have a proper name, but may also be referred to simply as "the god of the father," that is, the god of the male clan leader. The primary human concerns, in this setting, are economic and social. The deity is viewed, correspondingly, as follows: "First, its physical aspect: the [divine] father as engenderer of the child; the [divine] mother as giving birth to it. Second, the provider aspect: the father as provider for his family. Third, the protector and intercessor aspect. Fourth, the claim parents have upon their children for honor and obedience."[6] In sum, he writes, "the individual matters to God, God cares about him personally and deeply."[7]

But for Jacobsen this "personal religion" displays deeply problematic aspects. The individual, even in times of penitence,

> becomes so centrally important in the universe that he can monopolize God's attention, can involve God deeply and emotionally . . . , and before this onslaught of unlimited ego, the figure of God appears to shrink: no longer the awesome creator and ruler of the All, he dwindles to "the God of *my* salvation." As in love that is *only* need-love the beloved ceases to be a person in his own right and is seen only as a means of gratifying desires in the lover, so here God is in danger of becoming a mere instrument for relieving personal needs in one individual.[8]

It is in the tension between these two basic metaphors for deity — as august cosmic king, and as intimate clan parent — that Jacobsen identifies the rise of what he calls "the problem of the religious sufferer." In Mesopotamia this problem is addressed in "two remarkable works, *Ludlul bel nemeqi* ('Let me praise the expert') and the Babylonian Theodicy."[9] The

---

6. Jacobsen, *The Treasures of Darkness*, 158.
7. Jacobsen, *The Treasures of Darkness*, 147.
8. Jacobsen, *The Treasures of Darkness*, 150.
9. Jacobsen, *The Treasures of Darkness*, 162.

problem is addressed, of course, also in the book of Job. Here, as Jacobsen interprets God's address to Job,

> the personal, egocentric view of the sufferer — however righteous — is rejected. The self-importance which demands that the universe adjust to his needs, his righteousness, is cast aside, and the full stature of God as the majestic creator and ruler of the universe is reinstated. The distance between the cosmic and the personal, between God in his infinite greatness and mere individual man, is so great and so decisive that an individual has no rights, not even to justice.[10]

As Frost would say, the two extremes are indeed "too hard to comprehend at once."

Jacobsen's analysis of the cosmic high god and personal clan god metaphors for deity is a classic of ancient Near Eastern religious scholarship. And his assessment of their relative adequacy in relation to the problem of human suffering is as psychologically perceptive as it is existentially challenging. In my view, he is dead on target in proposing that the book of Job is to be read and interpreted in the context of the tension between these two metaphors. However, from this tension I will draw conclusions that in certain fundamental respects differ sharply from his. For now, we may consider one critique of his analysis that may open the way to such conclusions. I refer to Jacobsen's identification of the parental metaphor of deity as originating in the second millennium, following upon (and perhaps in reaction to) the royal cosmic metaphor that had become predominant in the third.

If religious imagery arises in relation to the concrete conditions of human life, one may question whether the royal cosmic imagery for deity arose prior to the parental. City-state forms of society, with kings at their head, did not precede forms of community proper to families and clans. Quite to the contrary. Families and clans, and eventually small un-walled villages where such groups established sedentary existence, preceded the development of walled cities and larger, more differentiated and stratified forms of society where ties between members of the community became political rather than kin-based. Where the language of kinship served to characterize city-state relationships, that language often functioned metaphorically: The "fatherly" relation of a king to his subjects was *likened to*

10. Jacobsen, *The Treasures of Darkness*, 163.

the relation of a biological father to his children. The "brotherly" relation of fellow citizens, or city-states in political covenant with one another, was *likened to* the relation of blood brothers. A city, in being called the "mother" of its citizens, was *likened to* a nurturing, protective mother of offspring. To say it again, then, if religious imagery arises in some correlation to the actual forms and concerns of human life, one would think that parental images of deity would arise prior to the emergence of royal imagery. In that case, one could view the upsurge of personal religion in the second millennium, not as a novel development, but as a reversion to and revival of forms and themes of religion that predated the third millennium but that had become overshadowed, and almost superseded, by the religious forms and themes of cosmic high god religion.

Such appears in fact to have been the case. Subsequent to the publication of Jacobsen's work, Robert Di Vito[11] has analyzed the personal names that are to be found among third-millennium writings unearthed by archaeologists. As he has shown, these names give abundant evidence that already in the fourth millennium the gods could be pictured as divine parents of the human family. The bearing of this on Jacobsen's analysis is manifold. At this point we may focus on one issue in that analysis. As we have seen, Jacobsen writes that "*before this onslaught* of unlimited ego [as expressed in personal religion], the figure of God appears to *shrink: no longer* the awesome creator and ruler of the All, he *dwindles* to 'the God of *my* salvation.'" In Jacobsen's view, the "default position" of the third millennium, with its image of the gods as cosmic rulers, becomes "customized" by *shrinking* the awesomeness of the divine creator and ruler and *dwindling* it to the personal god as "the God of *my* salvation." But if Di Vito is right, the reverse is the case. An earlier "default position," in which the worshipper enjoys a personal relation to the deity, is overwhelmed and displaced by the awesomeness of the divine creator and ruler. Indeed, elsewhere in his book, where he discusses the rise of the cosmic ruler metaphor, Jacobsen writes as follows of the divine king in his capacity as warrior-protector:

> [A] new savior-figure had come into being, the ruler: exalted above men, fearsome as warrior, awesome in the power at his command. . . .

---

11. Robert Di Vito, *Studies in the Third Millennium Sumerian and Akkadian Personal Names: The Designation and Conception of the Personal God.* Studia Pohl, series minor 16 (Rome: Pontifical Biblical Institute, 1993).

[T]his new concept of the ruler . . . provided an approach to central aspects of the Numinous [that is, to the divine] which had not been readily suggestible before: the aspects of tremendum as 'majesty' and 'energy.' In the small, tight-knit society of the village and small town, such as we must suppose for ancient Mesopotamia in the earliest period, there had not been much social differentiation between people, and not much opportunity for feelings of awe and reverence to develop. With the concentration of power in the person of the king, the experience of awe and majesty entered everyday experience.[13]

In light of Di Vito's analysis, we may, then, view the religious development as follows: (1) an initial experience and understanding of deity with the use of parental metaphors; (2) a subsequent understanding and experience of deity with the use of ruler metaphors which (corresponding to the way in which city-state politics supervened in the affairs of its citizens) took prominence over the earlier parental metaphors; (3) a revival, among some elements of the population, and in regard to at least some of its urgent concerns, of the parental metaphors, perhaps in reaction to the august, distant status of the high gods. In this new setting, the personal god might be a minor deity who could function as an intercessor on one's behalf in the heavenly realm — much like a lobbyist in Washington on behalf of a special interest group or a congressperson elected from one's local district. But a human king might have the divine cosmic ruler as his personal god. In any case, the problem of the religious sufferer emerged in Mesopotamian literature as a tension between these two metaphors.

Before we turn to the biblical story, we may note how Jacobsen concludes his discussion of Mesopotamian personal religion:

As far as we can see, it is only Israel that decisively extended the attitude of personal religion from the personal to the national realm. The relationship of Yahweh to Israel — his anger, his compassion, his forgiveness, and his renewed anger and punishment of the sinful people — is in all essentials the same as that of the relation between god and individual in the attitude of personal religion.[13]

12. Jacobsen, *The Treasures of Darkness*, 79.
13. Jacobsen, *The Treasures of Darkness*, 164.

If that is so — if the relationship of Yahweh to Israel is fundamentally "the relation between god and individual in the attitude of personal religion" — then the book of Job as Jacobsen interprets it stands closer to Mesopotamian religion on the question of human suffering than it does to the religion of Israel as set forth in the Old Testament. In Jacobsen's reading, both Mesopotamian religion and the book of Job resolve the issue of personal suffering by rejecting the personal religion model in favor of the cosmic high God model. I read Job differently. Like Jacobsen, I see this book as wrestling with human suffering in terms of the two metaphors of God as cosmic ruler and as clan parent. But as I read the book, it resolves the issue in terms of the personal-clan model. One indication of this, as we shall see, is the prominence of the divine name Shadday in Job, a divine name which otherwise occurs most prominently in relation to the ancestors of Genesis 12–50 and which is explicitly replaced by the name Yahweh in Exod 6:3.

Models of Divine-Human Relation in the Old Testament

Early in the book of Exodus, God is portrayed as saying something to Moses that is remarkable in its implications: "I am the Lord [that is, "Yahweh"]. I appeared to Abraham, to Isaac, and to Jacob, as God Almighty [El Shadday], but by my name the Lord I did not make myself known to them" (Exod 6:3). In the ancient world, a divine name is a fundamental indicator not only of the identity but also of the character of the deity. In the above case, the shift from "God Almighty," or El Shadday, to "the Lord," or "Yahweh," marks an epoch-making shift from one paradigm of divine-human relations to another. The shift is marked by dramatic new developments as well as important underlying continuities. The critical issue is, in what sense the new developments replace or supersede the old forms. In this chapter I will argue (as I have argued also in other writings) that the old paradigm (signaled here by the divine name El Shadday) sets forth the "original default position" of the divine-human relation, while the new paradigm (signaled here by the divine name, Yahweh) sets forth the "customized default position." That, certainly, is one way of characterizing the Apostle Paul's understanding of the Abrahamic and Mosaic paradigms as he discusses them in Galatians 3 and in Romans 4. But I do not intend to impose Paul's understanding on the discussion here. Rather, I want to show how the two paradigms, in their respective character and in their sequence, are illuminated when considered against the Mesopotamian background outlined in the previous section, and how they are related to one another in the unfolding of the biblical narrative.

Abraham and Family

As biblical scholars have come to recognize, the religion of Abraham and the other ancestors in Genesis 12–50 displays many of the features of personal (or family/clan) religion in Mesopotamia, and indeed in Canaan as well. Scholars have drawn attention to such items as the names of the Genesis ancestors, like "Abram" ("the [divine] father is exalted"), and the expression "the God of my/your/his father" (e.g., Exod 3:6). The concerns of the Genesis ancestors are primarily economic and revolve around the fertility of field, flock, and family. Issues of conception, birth, nurture, provision of lush pasture and watering places, and guidance to such places are paramount. Communal ethos — what gives the community its identity, its distinctive tone or flavor, and its cohesiveness amid strains that would pull it apart — is summed up in the Hebrew phrase *ḥesed we'ĕmet*, often translated as "steadfast love and faithfulness," that is, faithful, enduring loyalty to one's kin.

Correspondingly, the God of the ancestors typically acts in their lives in promising (and, often after some delay, enabling) conception and birth, and in leading the ancestors from place to place for fruitful land and pasturage. These core issues are summed up in Gen 49:25, as Jacob blesses the tribe of Joseph

> by the God of your father, who will help you,
> by Shadday who will bless you
> with blessings of heaven above,
> blessings of the deep that lies beneath,
> blessings of the breasts [*šādayim*] and of the womb [*reḥem*].

According to this text, Shadday, the "God of the father" (that is, the family or clan God, Jacobsen's "personal" God) is the giver of both cosmic and human fertility. (Note that Shadday is here both a personal God and a God of cosmic scope.) The "blessings of heaven above" are experienced in the rain that falls on the earth, and the "blessings of the deep" in the water that rises from underground sources, the water in both forms rendering the earth — as in Genesis 2 — fruitful. The analogy with the blessings of breasts and womb is patent.

Let us explore a number of the features in this text more fully, beginning with the divine name Shadday. The name occurs first in Gen 17:1-2, where God appears to Abram and says, "I am El Shadday; walk before me, and be blameless. And I will make my covenant between me and you, and will multiply you exceedingly." It occurs a second time in 28:3; here Isaac, sending Jacob off to Paddan-aram, blesses him, saying, "El Shadday bless you and make you fruitful and multiply you, that you may become a company of peoples." It occurs a third time in 35:11-12, as Jacob returns from that place and God says to him, "I am El Shadday: be fruitful and multiply; a nation and a company of nations shall come from you, and kings shall spring from you. The land which I gave to Abraham and Isaac I will give to you, and I will give the land to your descendants after you." It occurs a fourth time in 43:14 where, as Jacob prepares to send his sons back to Egypt for more grain, he offers this prayer: "may El Shadday grant you mercy [raḥămîm] before the man, that he may send back your other brother and Benjamin." It occurs a fifth time in 48:3-4; just before Jacob blesses Joseph's two sons in Egypt, he says to Joseph, "El Shadday appeared to me at Luz in the land of Canaan and blessed me, and said to me, 'Behold, I will make you fruitful, and multiply you, and I will make of you a company of peoples, and will give this land to your descendants after you for an everlasting possession.'" It occurs a sixth time in Genesis, as we have seen, in 49:25, where it appears only as Shadday. (In explicit reference to the ancestors it occurs, for the seventh and last time, in Exod 6:3.) Over the past century and more, scholars have analyzed the narratives in Genesis as a weaving together of a number of earlier strands of tradition. The texts quoted above, featuring the divine name (El) Shadday, are generally attributed to the so-called Priestly strand. But the creation story in Gen 1:1–2:3 is also attributed to this same strand. This means that, so far as the Priestly tradition is concerned, the personal God of the ancestors is one and the same God as the cosmic creator of Genesis 1. The ancestral stories in Genesis 12–50 may be said, then, to pick up and embody the themes of fruitfulness and blessing first announced in Gen 1:11-12; 1:22; and 1:28, and to sum up those themes in 49:25, just before Jacob's death in Egypt.

Second, let us notice the pun, in the way the Hebrew word for "breasts" *(šādayim)* echoes the divine name Shadday. In our day a pun is a low form of humor, of no more than passing and diverting interest. It carries no real weight of information or meaning. In the ancient world puns worked quite differently, often to give important new meaning to an old word, a meaning which would have consequences for the future. Often in Genesis, for example, an ancient name is given new meaning by associating it with a similar-sounding verb. Similarly, in Amos 5:5 the sentence "Gilgal shall go into exile" is given fatefully added force by a play on the place-name. *Gilgal* originally meant "circle of stones," from the verb *gālal,* "to roll." In this punning passage, however, it is associated with a similar verb, *gālâ,* "to go into exile." In the matter of the divine name Shadday, scholars are of differing minds on its original meaning. One common explanation associates it with a Mesopotamian word, *šad,* "mountain." In that case, one scholar ventures, Shadday may carry the same connotations as the name that French explorers gave to the mountain range we call the Grand Tetons ("great breasts"). Whatever the original meaning of the name Shadday, in Gen 49:25 the pun based on sound-similarity makes the present meaning clear: Shadday is the giver of the blessings of the *šad,* the breast.

But another Hebrew pun, or at least pun potential, lurks in this passage. The concrete noun *reḥem,* "womb," has as its cognates the abstract noun *raḥămîm,* "compassion, mercy," and the associated verb *raḥēm,* "to act compassionately, to show mercy." Just as *ḥesed* is the loyalty kin-folk are expected to show to one another, so *raḥămîm* is the compassion, the mercy, a mother owes to her children (see Isa 49:15) and children of the same womb *(reḥem)* owe to one another. So it is with a delicious dramatic irony, hidden from Jacob himself but evident to the reader, that Jacob prays, in Gen 43:14: "may El Shadday grant you mercy [*raḥămîm*] before the man, that he may send back your other brother and Benjamin." The irony is that Jacob does not know who "the man" is, and can only pray, in forlorn hope, that that man down there, whoever he is, will show compassion to the aliens coming before him. When the brothers do appear before Joseph, it is when his eyes fall on Benjamin, his one full brother among the group, that he exclaims, "God be gracious [*ḥānan*] to you, my son!" And his heart yearns (the Hebrew says, literally, his *raḥămîm* grows warm) for his brother (43:29-30). Shadday, giver of the blessings of *šad* and *reḥem,* is also giver of the blessings of *raḥămîm.*

We see the same scenario in other parts of the ancestral narrative. Jacob and Esau have become estranged over the way Jacob stole Esau's birthright and then his blessing from the aged Isaac. When, after many decades, they are about to meet again, Jacob prays to God as follows (Gen 32:9-12):

> O *God of my father Abraham* and *God of my father Isaac*, O Lord who didst say to me, "Return to your country and to your kindred, and I will do you good," I am not worthy of the least of all the steadfast love [*ḥesed*] and all the faithfulness [*'ĕmet*] which thou hast shown to thy servant, for with only my staff I crossed this Jordan; and now I have become two companies. Deliver me, I pray thee, from the hand of my brother, from the hand of Esau, for I fear him, lest he come and slay us all, the mothers with the children. But thou didst say [to Abraham! See Gen. 22:17], "I will do you good, and make your descendants as the sand of the sea, which cannot be numbered for multitude."

This prayer operates entirely within the ethos of personal/clan religion. Its aftermath, in Gen 33:1-11, is a deeply affecting scene of brotherly reconciliation.

Similarly, after the death of Jacob, his other sons, unsure of Joseph's attitude toward them now that the clan father is dead, approach him in penitence beseeching his forgiveness. The way they frame this request is telling. They begin by invoking the name of their father, who enjoined them to ask Joseph to forgive "the transgression of *your brothers*." And they end by asking him to forgive them as "the servants of *the God of your father*" (Gen 50:16-17). It is within this context that he responds favorably to their prayer. The *raḥămîm* that he had earlier felt toward his full brother Benjamin is now unambiguously extended to them. (We may recall Jacobsen's comment, as quoted above, according to which divine compassion for humans is a feature of the "personal," or familial, religious paradigm.)

Moses and Israel

When we follow the biblical story from Genesis into Exodus, at first we see God manifest in the same kind of divine activity as in the ancestral narratives. In Egypt "the descendants of Israel were fruitful and increased greatly; they multiplied and grew exceedingly strong; so that the land was filled with them" (Exod 1:7). This passage repeats the key terms not only of

Gen 1:28 but also of 17:2, 6, 16, 20, as well as 28:3; 35:11; and 48:4 — all passages in which God is identified as El Shadday. When Pharaoh responds to Israel's proliferation in the land with increasingly harsh measures of suppression, God responds through Israel's increasing fruitfulness (Exod 1:12, 20-21), an implicit sign of (El) Shadday's activity. And when, in response to the people's mounting groans and cries for help (2:23-25) God calls to Moses at the burning bush, it is as "the God of your father, the God of Abraham, the God of Isaac, and the God of Jacob" (3:6). To this point in the biblical story, the Abrahamic paradigm still holds good.

But then a remarkable transformation begins to transpire. When Moses says to God, "Who am I that I should go to Pharaoh, and bring the children of Israel out of Egypt?" (Exod 3:11), God says, "I will be [*'ehyeh*] with you [*'immāk*]" (3:12). To this, Moses responds, "If I come to the people of Israel and say to them, 'The God of your fathers has sent me to you,' and they ask me, 'What is his name?' what shall I say to them?" (3:13). Why does Moses ask this question? Does he not already know the answer, from God's self-identification a moment ago at the bush (3:6)? Why can't he say to them, "The God of your father, the God of Abraham, the God of Isaac, and the God of Jacob, has sent me"? In a number of places in Genesis, some version of this formula, or simply "the God of my/your/their father," has been deemed sufficient to identify the ancestral God (Gen 26:24; 31:5, 29, 42, 53; 43:23; 46:1, 3; 50:17). Why not here? One answer is that, to the Israelites in their present predicament in Egypt, God's presence and activity in the blessings of breast and womb is no help against the Egyptians. For it is the Israelites' increase in numbers that has led to the current crisis, and further blessing of this sort by the ancestral God will only make matters worse in provoking Pharaoh to ever harsher measures.

So God responds in words that inaugurate a theological revolution whose implications continue to reverberate down to our own day. God replies, "I AM WHO I AM" — at least, that is how English translators have rendered the Hebrew words (Exod 3:14). This follows the Latin translation, which itself may be influenced by the Greek translation, "I am the one who is." But the Hebrew words are *'ehyeh 'ăšer 'ehyeh*, and the verb *'ehyeh* in ordinary narrative contexts is most naturally translated "I will be." So, for example, in Gen 26:3 God says to Isaac, "Sojourn in this land, and I will be with you [*'ehyeh 'immĕkā*], and will bless you; for to you and to your descendants I will give all these lands, and I will fulfill the oath which I swore to Abraham your father." Here the verb is used to convey the promise of

God's presence and activity in the future, a presence and an activity connected with the concerns typical of religion in the ancestral paradigm. Similarly, in Gen 31:3 God says to Jacob, "Return to the land of your fathers and to your kindred, and I will be with you ['*ehyeh 'immāk*]." Now, when God says to Moses, "I will be with you ['*ehyeh 'immāk*], and Moses asks, in effect, "who are you?" God's response begins with that same '*ehyeh*. But then, instead of indicating some specific action or some specific divine characteristic, God continues with a mind-boggling '*ăšer 'ehyeh* — "who I will be"! So we may translate the whole response, "I will be who I will be," or, as suggested in the margin of NRSV, "I will be what I will be." It is as though God says to Moses, "I can be present and active in your midst not only as the kind of God who was manifest in the typical concerns of the ancestors and who is now manifest in the fruitfulness of their descendants in Egypt. I can be present and active in your midst in whatever fashion I decide, in appropriate response to whatever the situation is in the world."

It is not that God is simply a divine reflection of whatever the worldly situation becomes. Rather, God is the divine mystery inexhaustible by any of our specific names for God. But the mystery is not simply hidden away; the divine mystery is disclosed, revealed, in response to the changing situations in the world. "I will be who I will be" is first of all an affirmation of God in God's own self — a mystery that is hidden in the very act of being disclosed for what it is! But in the context of this disclosure to Moses at the bush, "I will be who I will be" is an affirmation of God's faithful responsiveness to the changing situations in the world. For "I will be who I will be" follows "I will be with you," and the whole scene at the burning bush comes in response to God's hearing, seeing, remembering of the ancestors, and knowing in Exod 2:23-25.

Then God says, "Tell them, ''*ehyeh* has sent me to you.'" But lest they think this '*ehyeh* is some strange new deity, God goes on to say, "Tell them, '*YHWH, the God of your fathers, the God of Abraham, the God of Isaac, and the God of Jacob, has sent me to you': this is my name for ever, and thus I am to be remembered throughout all generations" (3:15). The divine name *YHWH* ("the LORD") had occurred already throughout Genesis, and there, like Shadday, had been associated with the concerns of ancestral religion. Now, at the bush, Yahweh, by the sort of punning association that we see so often in Genesis, is given a new connotation. The ancestral God is one who is free to become whatever God chooses to become. But lest this be thought to identify God as merely arbitrary and capricious, in 3:15 this

God remains firmly connected to the ancestral tradition. If, hereafter, *YHWH* stands for *'ehyeh*, which in turn is short for *'ehyeh 'ăšer 'ehyeh*, nevertheless, says God to Moses, this *YHWH* faithfully remains "the God of your fathers." In changing (so far as the name changes), God remains faithfully the same. Indeed, insofar as the present crisis calls for God to act in new ways, only by changing can God remain faithfully the same.

Why this extraordinary care to clarify and redefine the divine name? It is because we are about to witness a dramatic shift in religious paradigms. In computer lingo, we are about to witness, in the book of Exodus as a whole, a shift from one default setting to another, a shift from what Walter Moberly calls "Patriarchal Religion" to what he calls "Mosaic Faith." And it is extraordinarily important not to make the mistake of thinking that in this shift the new default setting simply supersedes the old one, simply renders it obsolete. As we shall see, crises — "fatal system errors" — will occur, which will call for a reversion to fundamental aspects of the original paradigm if there is to be any future for the divine-human relation. If the move to the new paradigm in Exodus involved a simple trashing or deleting of the ancestral paradigm as obsolete and of no further use, such "fatal system errors" would leave Israel facing a dead end.

So important is this transition that it is negotiated again in Exodus 6. This time, issues that were implicit in the scene at the burning bush become explicit. There, God had spoken of Pharaoh releasing the Israelites under the compulsion of "a mighty hand" (*yad ḥăzāqâ*, 3:19). Now God reiterates that promise (6:1, where "strong hand" translates *yad ḥăzāqâ*). Then God says to Moses, "I am the Lord. I appeared to Abraham, to Isaac, and to Jacob, as God Almighty, but by my name the Lord I did not make myself known to them" (6:2-3). What does this mean? Has not the name YHWH appeared frequently in Genesis? Yes, but not with the new connotation given at the burning bush. In Gen 18:14 God had said to Sarah, "Is anything too hard [or "wonderful," Hebrew *yippālē'*) for the Lord?" In this ancestral setting, the measure of God's ability to do a wonderful thing was to assure Abraham that Sarah, at her age, would have a son. Now, in Exod 3:20 the calculus has changed. "I will stretch out my hand and smite Egypt with all the wonders [*niplĕ'ōt*] which I will do in it; after that he will let you go." As the story of the exodus will demonstrate in many ways, and as the song at the sea makes explicit, YHWH has now become "a man of war" (Exod 15:3). This is reinforced several times in those later biblical contexts where God is spoken of as "making a name for himself." In each instance

(Neh 9:10; Isa 63:12, 14; Jer 32:20; Dan 9:15), the divine action by which this occurs is the mighty deliverance of Israel from Egypt. Further, when God goes on to say to Moses, "I will take you for my people, and I will be your God" (Exod 6:7), this is shorthand for the covenant that Israel and God will enter into at Mount Sinai, a covenant sealed by solemn oaths and blood (Exod 24:3-8). Through this mighty deliverance and solemn covenant, God becomes Israel's divine King (Exod 15:18) and, as such, the giver of detailed laws, by observance of which Israel is to enact faithfulness to its covenant Lord and its members are to enact justice toward one another.

The paradigm shift is complete. Israel's relation to God rests now on a new default setting. The paradigm is now not familial-organic but political-contractual; God is now not simply Shadday, but YHWH understood as divine warrior and covenant lord. Formerly, the ethos of family relations simply called for *ḥesed* — "kin loyalty" — and it was unnecessary to spell that out in a prescribed list of behaviors. Clan custom was a sufficient guide to the claims of *ḥesed*. Again and again, in whatever sort of situation, it was necessary only to call for someone to (as the Hebrew expression goes) "do *ḥesed*" — show loyalty or kindness (Gen 19:19; 20:13; 21:23; 24:12; 32:10; 39:21; 40:14; 47:29) — and the specific character of the situation would indicate what *ḥesed* called for. Similarly, objections to behavior were not justified by appeal to laws, but simply by saying, "It is not so done in our country" (Gen 29:26) or "such a thing ought not to be done" (34:7). Now, with the covenant at Sinai, the call to serve God faithfully and observe justice within Israel was embodied in detailed laws. And these laws were backed up by sanctions — rewards for compliance and punishments for violation. (The most elaborate expression of these sanctions appears in Deuteronomy 28.) Relations which had gone wrong were now reestablished not simply on the basis of *raḥămîm,* but through an increasingly elaborate sacrificial procedure on the one hand and legal proceedings on the other. It is highly significant, in this connection, that the ancestral narratives are devoid of any reference to divine anger or wrath (one frequent Hebrew word for which is *'ap,* literally "nose, nostril"), though there is plenty of reference to persons angry with one another. But this aspect of God emerges hand-in-hand with the transition to the new paradigm (Exod 4:14; 15:8; 22:24; 32:10, 11, 12). And along with it emerges the theme of God's jealousy: "You shall have no other gods before me . . . ; for I the Lord your God am a jealous God, visiting the iniquity of the fathers upon the children to the third and the fourth generation of those who hate me, but showing steadfast love to thousands of those who love me and keep my commandments" (Exod 20:3-6).

After a Fatal System Error, Which Paradigm?

The commandment just quoted from the Decalog raises the question: How was fundamental covenant betrayal dealt with? When Israel, at the foot of Sinai and in the very shadow of its oaths of loyalty, corrupts itself in making the golden calf (Exod 32:8), the God of the covenant responds by saying to Moses, "I have seen this people, and behold, it is a stiff-necked people; now therefore let me alone, that my wrath may burn hot against them and I may consume them; but of you I will make a great nation" (32:9-10). By the terms of the covenant, minor and even serious offenses could be dealt with and reestablished through cultic and legal proceedings. But within the logic of this covenant, the fundamental rebellion of idolatry is so grave as to spell the end of the relation.

What does Moses do? Does he take up the divine offer? Or does he hear within it an implicit invitation to recall the ancestral paradigm? At the beginning of Israel's ancestral story, Abram had heard God say to him, "I will make of you a great nation" (Gen 12:2). It is as though God is extending to Moses the call earlier made to Abram. But what would be the point of taking up God's offer — of becoming, in effect, a second Abraham — only to see his multiplied descendants, somewhere down the line, go through their own analogy to Egyptian bondage, their own exodus deliverance, their own covenanting with God at some local equivalent to Sinai, only to have them come to a dead end in idolatry? And what kind of God would he be dealing with in such a case?

Moses takes another tack — a tack that I suspect God has solicited in echoing Gen 12:2 and thereby implicitly invoking the older paradigm. Moses intercedes on Israel's behalf. Now, as a way of dealing with the fundamental "fatal system error" of idolatry, the terms of the Sinai covenant, in Exodus 20–23, make no provision for intercession. Certainly Moses makes no appeal to any such provision. The heart of his intercession, as indicated by their climactic placement at the end of his intercession, comes in the words, "Turn from thy fierce wrath [*'ap*], and repent of this evil against thy people. Remember Abraham, Isaac, and Israel, thy servants, to whom thou didst swear by thine own self, and didst say to them, 'I will multiply your descendants as the stars of heaven, and all this land that I have promised I will give to your descendants, and they shall inherit it for ever'" (Exod 32:12-13). Moses' appeal is not to a provision in the Sinai covenant for such a crisis, but to the ethos of God's relation to the ancestors.

As a result, "the Lord repented of the evil which he thought to do to his people" (Exod 32:14). Like God's motivation for the exodus in the first place (Exod 2:24; 3:6, 15, 16; 4:5; 6:3, 8), God's motivation for sparing the people in the face of their fundamental covenant betrayal rests in the ancestral promise and covenant. This is to say that, in the face of the "fatal system error" of idolatry which occurs in the context of the "customized default setting" established by the Sinai covenant, God reverts to the "original default setting" established with Abraham — a setting which itself was of a piece with God's intention and provision for humankind in creation.

This is borne out by what follows in Exodus 33. To appreciate what transpires there, we need to reflect briefly on one aspect of the contrast between God and Pharaoh in the earlier chapter. When God had seen the Israelites' plight under Egyptian oppression, God had appeared to Moses in a new guise: No longer simply "giver of the blessings of breast and womb," God now became a divine warrior-deliverer and covenant Lord. In contrast, when Moses came to Pharaoh and interceded with him on behalf of the people, Pharaoh had hardened his heart against them and persisted in his established policies toward them. How would this covenant lord now respond to Moses' intercession to spare the people from the judgment that, by the logic of the Sinai covenant, was their just desert? Would this covenant lord be as intransigent as Pharaoh? Would this divine ruler harden his heart against Israel as Pharaoh had? Would that be the upshot, in this context, of the declaration, "I will be who I will be" — that God is free to ignore Moses' intercession, free to ignore the ethos of the relation with the ancestors, free to insist on the logic of the covenant and its sanctions?

Apparently not. When Moses intercedes, God — unlike Pharaoh — "turns" and "repents" of the threatened action (Exod 32:12-13). And this turning and repenting (or relenting) is grounded, once again, in a disclosure of who God is. For God says to Moses, "I will make all my goodness pass before you, and will proclaim before you the name, 'The Lord'; and I will be gracious to whom I will be gracious, and I will show mercy on whom I will show mercy" (33:19). The Hebrew verbs here are significant. The first one is ḥānan, "be gracious," encountered already, along with its noun cognate, in Genesis (32:5; 33:5, 8, 10, 11; and note esp. Gen 43:29). The second one is *raḥēm*, "show compassion, have mercy," an action grounded in tender warm feeling such as a mother shows her children, and (as we saw in Gen 43:30) such as children of the same mother are to show one another. In Hebrew the connective word "and" can introduce a clause that interprets or spells out what went before it. Some recent interpreters of this passage, accordingly, translate the latter part of the verse: "I will proclaim before you the name, 'The Lord,' to wit: 'I will be gracious to whom I will be gracious, and I will show mercy on whom I will show mercy.'" That is to say, in the face of Israel's fundamental betrayal of the Sinai covenant, and in view of the logic of that covenant which would entail a dead end for Israel for idolatry, YHWH who "will be who I will be" becomes YHWH who "will be gracious to whom I will be gracious, and will show mercy on whom I will show mercy." This is not a statement of God's freedom to be merciful to some and not to others. It is a statement of God's freedom from the kind of statecraft-grounded logic of a Pharaoh who can harden his heart against Israel to the point where he cannot unharden it — the logic of a Pharaoh trapped inside his own unrelenting logic. It is a statement of God's freedom to step back from the logic of the Sinai covenant with its strict sanctions, back from the inevitability of divine wrath, and to act in the spirit of the Shadday in whose name Jacob invoked compassion on his sons and Joseph enacted it toward them. And this is not a onetime, *ad hoc* response to Moses' intercession. For in Exod 34:6-7 the adjectives formed from these verbs introduce a passage that discloses the settled character of God:

> The Lord, the Lord, a God merciful [*raḥûm*] and gracious [*ḥannûn*],
> slow to anger [*'erek 'appayim*, literally, "long of nostrils"],
> and abounding in steadfast love and faithfulness [*ḥesed we'ĕmet*],
> keeping steadfast love [*ḥesed*] for thousands,
> forgiving iniquity and transgression and sin,
> but who will by no means clear the guilty,
> visiting the iniquity of the fathers upon the children and the
> children's children, to the third and the fourth generation.

The Sinai covenant is to be reestablished (Exod 34:1-4); and it will operate once again as the "customized default setting" for Israel's relation to God. Moreover, the fundamental covenant betrayal of idolatry will continue to entail grave consequences. (We should note that the language of "visiting the iniquities of the fathers upon the children" appeared in 20:5 in specific reference to idolatry and that it probably has the same specific reference here.) Yet those consequences are to be borne within the bosom, as it were, of the proclamation of God's fundamental character as set forth in the opening lines of this passage.

As we shall see, the opening clauses of the proclamation in Exod 34:6 recur again and again throughout the Old Testament; and they reappear in various ways in the New Testament as well. Given the fact that the (re-newed) Sinai covenant becomes the "customized default setting" through-out the rest of the Old Testament, and given the fact that this proclamation of God as merciful and gracious introduces the scene in which that cov-enant is renewed (in Exodus 34), it is easy to gain the impression that this proclamation is integral to the Sinai covenant and its logic. If that is so, it is because the logic of the Sinai covenant, with its life-or-death sanctions, has become tempered by the compassionate ethos of the ancestral paradigm. And where the Sinai covenant, so to speak, "loses its temper" in the face of Israel's rebellions and idolatries, Israel's continuation before God turns on a reversion to the ethos of the ancestors.

This analysis resembles the conclusion that Thorkild Jacobsen leaves us with at the end of his chapter on personal religion:

> The relationship of Yahweh to Israel — his anger, his compassion, his forgiveness, and his renewed anger and punishment of his sinful people — is in all essentials the same as that of the relation between god and in-dividual in the attitude of personal religion. With this understanding of national life and fortunes as lived under ultimate moral responsibility, Israel created a concept of history as purposive — one which in basic es-sentials still governs conceptions of meaningful historical existence.[14]

The one element in this passage from which I would demur is the way Jacobsen has sequenced his terms: anger, compassion, forgiveness, and re-newed anger and punishment. Granted, the Old Testament as a whole is replete with terms and descriptions of God as wrathful. But as I have al-ready observed, these terms come into play primarily within those parts of the biblical story governed by the Sinai covenant paradigm. In a paradigm in which God is giver of conception, birth, nurture, guidance and protec-

14. Jacobsen, *The Treasures of Darkness,* 164.

tion and the divine source and sanction for the kin virtues of *ḥesed* and *raḥămîm*, God is *first* a God of compassion. Even where the ancestors grievously violate one another, God is almost distressingly "slow to anger" (to quote Exod 34:6-7). As Leo Tolstoy put it in one of his short stories, in the face of human wrongdoing "God knows, and he waits." And this divine forbearance, or patience, has its counterpart in the patience that various persons in Genesis are called on to exercise, not only in relation to the divine promises, but also in relation to the animosities of other persons.

3. Tracing the Pattern Elsewhere in the Bible

In the preceding chapter, I have argued that Israel's "default position" before God is to be distinguished in terms of an "original position" and a "customized position" and that, when Israel's relation with God within the customized position of the Sinai covenant suffers a "fatal system error," God does not allow matters to come to a dead end but carries them forward by reversion to the original default position. The first dramatic instance of this reversion comes, as we have seen, in Exodus 32–34, where the idolatry of the golden calf threatens to bring Israel to a dead end under the enforcement of the sanctions of the Sinai covenant, but where Israel is spared as a people through the intercession of Moses in which he invokes God's relation to the ancestors.

We see a crisis of similar gravity, with the same strategy of resolution, in Numbers 13–14. There, the people fear to go up into the land that was promised to them, persuaded by the majority of the spies that the people in that land "are stronger than we." So fearful are they that they resolve to choose another leader and return to Egypt (Num 13:31; 14:1-4). But this is another form of idolatry, for it implies that the gods of these people are stronger than YHWH their God (contrast Exod 12:12). God's response is essentially like God's response to the golden calf: to disinherit them and make of Moses a great and mighty nation (Num 14:11-12). As in Exod 32:11-13, Moses intercedes on behalf of the people. This time, instead of directly invoking God's covenant relation with the ancestors, Moses concludes his prayer by invoking the words that God had spoken to him in Exod 34:6-7:

> Let the power [kōaḥ] of the Lord *be great* as thou hast promised, saying, 'The Lord is slow to anger, and abounding in steadfast love, forgiving in-

iquity and transgression, but he will by no means clear the guilty, visiting the iniquity of fathers upon children, upon the third and upon the fourth generation.' Pardon the iniquity of this people, I pray thee, according to *the greatness* of thy steadfast love [*ḥesed*], and according as thou hast forgiven this people, from Egypt even until now. (Num 14:17-19)

It is instructive to note how the word *kōaḥ* ("power, strength, might) is used here, in comparison with its occurrences in Genesis and in Exodus. In Genesis, *kōaḥ* occurs three times: in reference to the productivity of the earth (4:12); in reference to Jacob's work as a shepherd for his father-in-law (31:6); and in Jacob's reference to Reuben, his first-born son, as "my might [*kōaḥ*], and the first fruits of my strength" (42:3). In these contexts, the word carries primarily reproductive and economic connotations. In the new paradigm inaugurated under Moses, God's great power manifested itself definitively in the acts by which God delivered Israel from Egypt. It is with these connotations that the word *kōaḥ* occurs in Exod 9:16; 15:6; 32:11. As in Moses' intercession in Exod 32:11, so here in Numbers Moses begins by appealing to God to remember how God brought the people out of Egypt "in your might [*kōaḥ*]" (Num 14:13). Then, however, Moses dramatically shifts the connotation of this word: In Num 14:17-19, God's "great" power is presented as the power of God to act in *ḥesed,* a *ḥesed* that in the present circumstance manifests itself in pardoning the iniquity of the people. That this power of forgiveness is rooted in the old default setting of ancestral religion is implicit in the fact that it is grounded in the divine character proclaimed in Exod 34:6-7. It becomes explicit in God's response to Moses, in that Israel in the form of its next generation (along with Caleb the one faithful spy) will "see the land which I swore to give to their fathers" (Exod 14:23). In passing, we may note how Moses' intercession is picked up in the Book of Common Prayer, where the Collect for the Sunday closest to September 28 opens with the words "O God, you declare your almighty power chiefly in showing mercy and pity." If that prayer, and Numbers 14, rightly identify the greatness of God's power, we may wonder whether the notions of divine power that inform so much of our religious understanding of God as "Almighty" are not in fact idolatrous!

When the book of Deuteronomy recaps the two crises in Exodus 32–34 and Numbers 13–14, it makes the ancestral basis of the latter resolution even more explicit. For while Moses' intercession in Exodus 32 is summarized simply in terms of his prostration and fasting before God for forty days, his intercession in Numbers 14 is similarly summarized and then followed by the words of his intercession:

> O Lord God, destroy not thy people and thy heritage, whom thou hast redeemed through thy greatness, whom thou hast brought out of Egypt with a mighty hand. *Remember thy servants, Abraham, Isaac, and Jacob;* do not regard the stubbornness of this people, or their wickedness, or their sin, lest the land from which thou didst bring us say, "Because the Lord was not able to bring them into the land which he promised them, and because he hated them, he has brought them out to slay them in the wilderness." For they are thy people and thy heritage, whom thou didst bring out by thy great power and by thy outstretched arm. (Deut 9:26-29)

As in Exodus 3, God's deliverance of the people from Egypt is rooted in God's relation to the ancestors, and so is Moses' plea for the forgiveness of their descendants. (One is reminded of the way Joseph's brothers invoke the name of their father Jacob and the God of their father in seeking his forgiveness in Genesis 50.)

Indeed, even though the book of Deuteronomy as a whole takes the form of a series of sermons in which Moses lays out the terms of the Sinai covenant, it is striking to note that the theme of God's promises to the ancestors runs like a golden thread throughout the book, occurring more than thirty times. It is not surprising, then, that even though this book presents the sanctions of the Sinai covenant in starkly elaborated terms (Deuteronomy 28), and even though the "either/or" of this covenant is reiterated powerfully again in 30:15-20 in terms of good and evil, life and death, blessing and curse, the last words of Moses in ch. 33 come not as such an either/or, but as an undialectical "yes" in the form of an unqualified blessing on the people. And if his immediately preceding song, in ch. 32, takes the form of a stern indictment of the people's idolatry with ensuing severe judgment on them, even here the divine-human relation is fundamentally imaged in terms of the relation between parent and child (32:4-6, 10-14, 18-19). It is this fundamental relation that is the ground of that song's positive ending.

In reading onward in the Old Testament, we will, to be sure, find Israel typically in the "customized default position" first established at Sinai. And we will eventually come to the establishment of yet another "customized default position," in the form of God's covenant with David. As scholars have shown, this covenant with David is itself rooted in the ancestral traditions. (One indication of this comes in Psalm 72, where the celebration of God's Davidic king concludes with a prayer that his name may endure for ever and that all people may bless themselves by him, all nations call him blessed — a clear echo of Gen 12:1-3.) But where Israel's standing before God comes in jeopardy through their idolatries and injustices, rendering them liable to that covenant's extreme sanctions, repeatedly we see an appeal to the ancestral relation as grounds for mitigation of the judgment.

So, for instance, when the king of Syria oppresses Israel, we read that "the Lord *was gracious* to them and *had compassion* on them, and he turned toward them, because of his covenant with Abraham, Isaac, and Jacob, and would not destroy them; nor has he cast them from his presence until now" (2 Kgs 13:23). Given what we have noted in Deut 9:26-29, it is not surprising that this biblical historian whose theology scholars have called "Deuteronomistic" should refer to the ancestors as the basis on which God YHWH "was gracious to them and had compassion on them" — the two verbs we encountered in Exod 33:19. When the northern kingdom falls before Assyria and goes into exile, it is in response to the ancestress Rachel that Jeremiah hears God's response of grace, based on the analogy of compassion [*raḥămîm*] for a wayward son (Jer 31:15-20). When Micah proclaims the judgment of God on Jerusalem, he nevertheless holds out hope for a subsequent restoration on the basis of God's character shown in Exod 34:6-7 and grounded in the ancestors (Mic 7:18-20). In the exile, the anonymous prophet-poet whom we call Deutero-Isaiah (Isaiah 40–55) repeatedly appeals to the ancestors as the basis of God's restoration (Isa 41:8-10; 51:1-3). Indeed, the figure of the Suffering Servant in Isaiah 53, which emerges as a sort of climax to Deutero-Isaiah's vision, may be introduced in the same connection. For the figure who grew up before God "like a young plant,/and like a root out of dry ground" (Isa 53:2) is reminiscent of Isaac, who was born late in the life of a woman who was considered barren. (On dry ground as an image for barrenness, see Prov 30:15-16. A fertile woman can be imaged as a well, and it is no surprise to observe how often, in the Bible, future bride and groom meet at a well.)

After the return from exile, when the Second Temple is being erected, Ezra (in Nehemiah 9) offers a long prayer of confession, recounting the history of Israel's rebellions and unfaithfulness, and celebrating again and again God's continual "great mercies" — a refrain that in Neh 9:17 quotes Exod 34:6-7. This whole recital and confession is grounded on the one hand in God as creator (Neh 9:6) and on the other hand in God's relation to

Abraham (9:7). It is in faithfulness to this relation that God has dealt graciously with a people rebellious from the time of Moses to Ezra's own day.

In addition to these references to the ancestors by name, we may note the frequency with which the leading terms of Exod 34:6 appear throughout the Old Testament: Deut 4:31; Ps 78:38; 86:15; 103:8; 111:4; 112:4; 145:8; Joel 2:13; Jonah 4:2. Psalm 103 is particularly noteworthy. For while it celebrates God's steadfast love *(ḥesed)* upon those who keep the covenant and remember to observe its commandments (103:17-18), it dwells most fully on God's forgiveness of iniquity (vv. 3, 9-12). And it grounds that forgiveness in the fact that God "made known his ways to Moses, his acts to the people of Israel. The Lord is merciful and gracious, slow to anger and abounding in steadfast love" (vv. 7-8), concluding that "as a father pities his children, so the Lord pities those who fear him. For he knows our frame; he remembers that we are dust" (vv. 13-14). As I noted in the previous chapter, the image of parental compassion appears again (this time in maternal terms) in Isa 49:15: "Can a woman forget her sucking child, that she should have no compassion on the son of her womb? Even these may forget, yet I will not forget you."

Let us return for a moment to Psalm 103. In the preceding chapter, I quoted words by Thorkild Jacobsen on the limits of personal religion, especially in connection with the book of Job. In part, he says: "The distance between the cosmic and the personal, between God in his infinite greatness and mere individual man, is so great and so decisive that an individual has no rights, not even to justice."[1] But in this psalm, the distance between the cosmic and the personal is precisely the measure of God's *ḥesed;* for,

> as the heavens are high above the earth,
> so great is his steadfast love toward those who fear him;
> as far as the east is from the west,
> so far does he remove our transgressions from us. (Ps 103:11-12)

Readers will decide for themselves whether in such a passage the sense of God "appears to shrink," as Jacobsen puts it,[2] or whether the sense of God as divine parent is awesomely magnified.

---

1. Thorkild Jacobsen, *The Treasures of Darkness* (New Haven: Yale University Press, 1976) 163.

2. Jacobsen, *The Treasures of Darkness,* 150.

The writers of the New Testament in various ways similarly ground the gospel message in God's relation to the ancestors. Without exploring all the relevant passages, I may simply list several of the more prominent texts: Matt 1:2; 3:9; 8:11; Mark 12:26; Luke 1:55, 73; 16:23-29; 19:9; John 8; Romans 4; Galatians 3. We may note also how Exod 34:6 is carried forward into John 1:14, 17, while Exod 33:19 forms the central text in Paul's long, tortured argument in Romans 9–11. For Paul quotes Exod 33:19 in Rom 9:15; and although in 9:18 he interprets it to mean "he has mercy upon whomever he wills, and he hardens the heart of whomever he wills," in 11:32 Paul comes to a different, radically inclusive conclusion: "God has consigned all to disobedience, that he may have mercy upon all." The basis for this shift in his interpretation of Exod 33:19, in moving from 9:18 to 11:32, is given in 11:25-28. Just as Paul had written of the hardening of Pharaoh's heart in 9:17-18, so he writes in 11:25 of the hardening that has come upon Israel: "As regards the gospel they are enemies of God" (11:28a). Not that they are the objects of God's enmity, but, like Paul himself at one time, they deny the claim that Jesus is God's promised and Israel's expected Messiah. Nevertheless, "as regards election they are beloved for the sake of their forefathers" (11:28b). In this long argument, we may say that Paul shows how he has "gone to school" in the sacred writings of his people and drawn a decisive distinction between the "original default setting" of God's relation to the ancestors and the "customized default setting" at Sinai which (as he puts it in Galatians 3) came in later.

Turning, Finally, toward Job

It is common for interpreters of the book of Job to read it as a critique of the theology of strict rewards and punishments typified by the book of Deuteronomy. So, for example, in "A Masque of Reason," his long poem on Job, Robert Frost has God thank Job in heaven "for releasing me/From moral bondage to the human race." God thanks him in particular for "the part you played/To stultify the Deuteronomist/And change the tenor of religious thought."[3] What I have attempted to do, in this chapter, is to lay the groundwork for my interpretation of how this comes about in Job. I will argue that the "change in religious thought" is not a new development, but

3. *Collected Poems, Prose, & Plays* (New York: Library of America, 1995) 245.

a reversion to the more fundamental paradigm of divine-human relations that this chapter has identified in the ancestral stories. Indeed, as my above comments on Deuteronomy already suggest, it is a mistake to characterize the book of Deuteronomy as merely propounding a theology of rewards and punishments. It is more true to say that Job plays an indispensable role in stultifying those interpretations of Deuteronomy that focus only on its exposition of the Sinai covenant and that overlook its frequent and many-faceted appeals to the ancestors.

The book of Job is variously dated. Many scholars place its composition in the period following the return of exiles from Babylon. Others date it within the period of the exile itself. Without going into all the issues here, I will simply indicate my own judgment that Job is exilic. During the exile, it is evident that a great many Israelites found the terms of the Sinai covenant to be powerfully explanatory of their plight. Israel had fallen into such grave and repeated violation of this covenant that the calamities of invasion by the armies of Babylon, destruction of cities and towns, ravaging of the countryside, and deportation of the leading figures of Jerusalem and Judea were deserved and unavoidable. As God put it to Jeremiah, even the intercessions of a Moses or a Samuel would not avert the coming calamity (Jer 15:1).

But the maelstrom of the exile caught up many innocent people in its path. And though the problem of innocent suffering was by no means new (it is as old as Abel), in this context it came to intensified expression. Both Jeremiah and Ezekiel addressed what apparently became a proverbial complaint: "The fathers have eaten sour grapes, and the children's teeth are set on edge" (Jer 31:29; Ezek 18:2). Ezekiel's response was to refine the doctrine of rewards and punishments so that, despite the terms of Exod 20:5, innocent persons would not suffer for the sins of their forebears. Nor would transgressors, despite the terms of Exod 20:6, be able to ride on the coattails of their forebears' righteousness. Each individual would receive from God the treatment appropriate to that person's ethical character (Ezek 18:5-24). For "the soul that sins shall die" (18:4) — only the soul that sins shall die, and that soul shall surely die.

Enter Job. Of course, he is not presented as a contemporary to the exiles (or to those who have returned from exile), but as one who lived in another time and in another place. But one may wonder what reverberations would arise within the minds and hearts of the first hearers and readers at the mention of the Chaldean raiders who stole Job's camels and killed his servants (Job 1:17). And would the great wind that came across the desert (that is, from the east) and destroyed the house in which his children were feasting, killing them all (1:19), conjure up in their minds also the prophetic pronouncements in which the Babylonians (aka Chaldeans) were imaged as a destructive east wind coming across the desert (Jer 4:11-12; 13:24; 18:17)? Like Job, there were those in Judah who could well be described as "blameless and upright, who feared God and turned away from evil" (Job 1:1). Their suffering in the exile was bad enough; but to have that suffering labeled as deserved by a clumsy application of the Deuteronomic theology or its individualizing refinement by Ezekiel was to add insult to injury and to compound the suffering. For all its importance in the biblical narrative, as a means to social order and justice and as a means to the interpretation of certain kinds of experience, that theology itself, as applied in this way, underwent a "fatal system error." The painfulness of this process, and its outcome, is traced in the book of Job, to which we will turn in the chapters that follow.

Meanwhile, I will conclude this chapter with three quotations that in one way or another image what I have been calling the original default position. The first quotation is from John Bowlby, *A Secure Base: Parent-Child Attachment and Healthy Human Development.*

> An ordinary devoted mother provides a child with a secure base from which he can explore and to which he can return when upset or frightened. . . . This concept, of the secure personal base, from which a child, an adolescent, or an adult goes out to explore and to which he returns from time to time, is one I have come to regard as crucial for an understanding of how an emotionally stable person develops and functions *all through his life.*[4]

The second quotation is a remark by Emily Dickinson in conversation with a friend: "Could you tell me what home is. I never had a mother. I suppose a mother is one to whom you hurry when you are troubled."[5] The third is from Robert Frost's poem "The Death of the Hired Man." The scene is one in which a long-time hired hand had left the farm to work for

---

4. (New York: Basic Books, 1988) 46.

5. Quoted in Cynthia Griffin Wolff, *Emily Dickinson* (New York: Alfred A. Knopf, 1986) 45.

someone else, but now has returned. The farm wife, seeing the man's condition, ventures that he has returned to this familiar place to die, as the nearest thing he has to a home. At this point the husband and wife engage in a short exchange on what home means. When the husband says, "Home is the place where, when you have to go there,/They have to take you in," the wife replies, "I should have called it/Something you somehow haven't to deserve."[6]

6. Frost, *Collected Poems, Prose, & Plays,* 43.

4. Trying to Grasp with Hand and Mind

In the preceding chapter I identified two paradigms, or models, of divine-human relation. Both of them existed in the ancient Near East prior to the rise of Israel and then persisted in these countries alongside Israel. Though I have summarized only the Mesopotamian form of these paradigms, as presented by Thorkild Jacobsen, subsequent studies by others have traced them also in Canaan. Before we move into the book of Job, it will be helpful to summarize them.

One paradigm is based on the structure and dynamics of family or clan relations and may be called a "kinship" paradigm. The other is based on the structure and dynamics of political relations (in that world, organized around a royal figure) and may be called a "covenant" paradigm. The "kinship" model is organic in nature, arising through birth, implicit in its values and claims, and persisting through the honoring of blood ties in acts of loyalty, generosity, and kindness. The "covenant" model arises where population has become so dense, and social relations so complex, that the bonds of kinship are insufficient. Here, the bonds of relation are established through explicit acts of covenanting choice and commitment and are sustained through observance of laws that have been promulgated and accepted.

In the Bible these two models are associated with the figures of Abraham and Moses. In the time of the ancestors, God is known as divine father of the clan. (As we saw, Abram's name means "the [divine] father is exalted.") Beginning with the exodus and the covenant at Sinai, God becomes known as Israel's Lord and King, delivering the people from Egypt and its oppressive laws and establishing new, just laws, the observance of which will be life-sustaining (Deut 6:20-25). I have likened each of these two models to the default settings on a computer. And I have proposed that the Abrahamic or kinship model is like the default settings installed at the factory, while the Mosaic or political/royal covenant model is like the default settings subsequently established by the "users" — in this instance, God and Israel at Sinai. Henceforth, the relations between God and Israel would be governed by the terms of the Sinai covenant.

Given the prominence of the Sinai covenant throughout the rest of the Old Testament, the impression could be gained that now the older kinship model was superseded and rendered obsolete — like a museum piece of interest to those who wished to indulge an appetite for ancient history or life in former times but now existing "behind glass" and no longer usable. However, Frank Moore Cross, in his study of Israelite religion, *Canaanite Myth and Hebrew Epic,* writes that "the covenant relation is properly described as a substitute kinship relation."[1] And in a later work, *From Epic to Canon: History and Literature in Ancient Israel,* in an essay entitled "Kinship and Covenant in Ancient Israel," he quotes George Mendenhall, who writes, "As social units become larger, kinship ties become increasingly dysfunctional as the basis for the larger group; but kinship terminology seems to become *more used* to express the new bond that ties the larger group together."[2] Cross goes on to observe that

> The language of kinship . . . is put to use even in parity treaties and vassal treaties negotiated at the international level between independent states. That such language survives in societies evolved far beyond the tribal level is remarkable, and it points to the tenacity of the kinship ethos, especially in peoples of the West Semitic world. . . . Often it has been asserted that the language of "brotherhood" and "fatherhood," "love," and "loyalty" is "covenant terminology." This is to turn things upside down. The language of covenant, kinship-in-law, is taken from the language of kinship, kinship-in-flesh.[3]

1. Frank Moore Cross, *Canaanite Myth and Hebrew Epic* (Cambridge, MA: Harvard University Press, 1973) 257-58.

2. Frank Moore Cross, *From Epic to Canon: History and Literature in Ancient Israel* (Baltimore: Johns Hopkins University Press, 1998) 7, quoting George E. Mendenhall, *The Tenth Generation: The Origins of the Biblical Tradition* (Baltimore: Johns Hopkins University Press, 1973) 177 (italics Cross's).

3. Cross, *From Epic to Canon,* 10-11.

As these remarks indicate, the concerns, values, and language of the earlier paradigm persist in some fashion even as the society adopts a new paradigm.

But what happens when the language of kin relations becomes merely formal rhetoric, mere window-dressing on the actuality of political covenant relations? What happens when the secondary model becomes in fact primary, when for all practical purposes the customized default setting becomes the original default setting? What happens when the logic of the law becomes so ingrained in people's psyches as to shape their ethos? And what happens when crises in covenant relations are dealt with only within that legal ethos?

Cross quotes Meyer Fortes, who writes, "Kinship predicates the axiom of amity, the prescriptive altruism exhibited in the ethic of generosity. . . . Kinfolk are expected to be loving, just, and generous to one another and not to demand strictly equivalent terms of one another."[4] What happens if the logic of the law becomes so deeply ingrained in their hearts (Deut 6:6-9; 11:18-21; 30:11-14) that people, forgetting other dimensions of the tradition, come to interpret their experience of weal and woe in "strictly equivalent terms," so that every good thing that happens is interpreted as a sign of divine approval and reward and every bad thing that happens is taken as evidence of divine disapproval and punishment? The book of Job shows us, at painful length, what can happen.

Job and His Family; God and His Court

The book opens with an idyllic portrayal of Job as an upright and devout, prosperous clan father — an ancient prototype of Ben Cartwright, the American cattle rancher in the TV series *Bonanza*. In every respect Job's life is a bonanza. As his name implies, his bonanza is the gift to him of the clan God of whom his name is a standing invocation. (Hebrew *iyyob* is apparently a development from an earlier form, *ayya-ab*, "where is the [divine] father?" — a name similar in substance to "Abram," *ab-ram*.) This idyllic opening scene is captured in all its transitory poignancy in the lyrical opening section of Ralph Vaughan Williams's musical composition *Job: A Masque for Dancing*.

4. Meyer Fortes, *Kinship and the Social Order: The Legacy of Lewis Henry Morgan* (Chicago: Aldine, 1969) 237, quoted in Cross, *From Epic to Canon*, 5-6.

The scene then shifts from earth to heaven, where all the members of the divine court have come to appear before Yahweh. Among them appears the Satan: "the Satan," not "Satan," for the word *haśśāṭān* here is apparently a common noun, prefixed by the definite article, designating the function of this figure, as when we say "the D.A." or "the County Prosecutor." Apparently the function of the Satan on behalf of the heavenly court is to go to and fro in the earth and to walk up and down in it, as "the eyes and ears of the king." One may compare him to Scanlon, in the old sitcom *Barney Miller,* who works for Internal Affairs in the New York police department. Those familiar with this TV series will recall Scanlon's periodic visits to Barney Miller's precinct headquarters, hoping to catch Miller or one of his officers red-handed in some piece of graft or corruption, some street-corner pay-off. Scanlon is totally dedicated to law and order. He is so obsessively dedicated to the workings of its logic that he derives his satisfaction from catching violators and setting in motion the inexorable workings of its punishments. And what drives his investigatory energies is a thoroughgoing suspicion that all police are "on the take" and that the greater the appearance of "good cop," the greater the likelihood of "bad cop."

So when Yahweh draws Scanlon's — that is, the Satan's — attention to Job as an exemplary citizen of God's realm on earth, the Satan responds suspiciously, "Is Job pious for nothing?" According to the Satan, Job is loyal to God because it pays off. Or rather, Job is loyal to God in grateful response for God's blessings upon him of prosperity and protection. Of course, on this point the Satan is right. Job's piety is the piety of gratitude. Just as an infant is bound to its mother, and in due course to its father, by ties of gratitude for nourishment and other forms of care, so, for example, Cain and Abel respond to God's blessings of the fruits of field and flock with return offerings in kind — offerings of gratitude, or thank-offerings. Such, it would appear, is the significance of a good many of the sacrificial scenes in Genesis 12–50. Abraham builds an altar at Shechem in response to God's promise of land to him (Gen 12:6-7). He builds another by the oaks of Mamre at Hebron, in response to another such promise (13:18). Jacob responds to God's promises to him by anointing a pillar at Bethel and vowing, "of all that you give me I will give the tenth to you" (28:22) In the context of kin relations, whether between humans or between humans and God, gratitude arises as a natural, organic response to generosity. And if such a grateful response assumes the continuation of divine blessing and favor, this is only to say that the ethos of family relations is an ethos of reciprocal generosity flowing back and forth within the bosom of mutual trust.

But the Satan sees Job's moral and religious response in different terms. As I read the Satan, his dedication to the divine King, and his preoccupation with observance and enforcement of the law that governs human affairs, have entered so deeply into his soul that he is suspicious of any talk of "generosity" on the one hand or "gratitude" on the other. He has come to view and to understand all interactions as motivated and choreographed only by the logic of *quid pro quo*, tit for tat, calculated exchange in "strictly equivalent terms." So the Satan asserts that Job is loyal to God and upright in his dealings with others, not simply out of gratitude, but out of an implicit calculation that his loyalty will guarantee God's continued blessing on him — not as a free, generous gift, but as what God will owe to him for his loyalty, in present-day terms a "kick-back." The proof of this, in the Satan's eyes, is that if God removes all these blessings Job will turn and curse God in the face.

What does God do? God could simply tell the Satan that he is wrong — that God can read Job's heart more deeply than the Satan can. That would spare Job all the terrible sufferings to follow. But of course, that would also deprive us of the help that this book may ultimately offer us in the sufferings that fall on us. For it would leave us at the mercy of those who, like the Satan, would read all that happens in terms of a strict system of rewards and punishments and would move them, and perhaps ourselves, to interpret all our sufferings as palpable evidence of our own moral and religious shortcomings.

If God were to answer the Satan's accusations on behalf of Job, that would also deprive Job of the right and the responsibility to speak for himself. In so doing, it would keep Job at a certain level of moral and religious immaturity. But the Satan's accusations against Job are also implicit accusations against God, for they imply that God is worthy of worship only for what we receive from God, and not for who God is simply as God. And what would God's naked assertions of his intrinsic worshipfulness prove, in the absence of Job's testimony? How can God break through the Satan's mind-set of strict *quid pro quo* and show that the divine-human relation is not simply locked within that logic, a logic that stifles all generosity, all freedom, on God's side *and* on Job's, and reduces everything to calculation and necessity?

I take God to be engaging in an act of dire, risky generosity, for God puts the whole case in Job's hands. I remember reading somewhere, decades ago, that in the Bible God is never the subject of the verb "to hope." The author's point, as I recall it, was that humans hope but God does not need to hope because God knows all outcomes. (This view, of course, brushes aside the implications of God's "*now* I know" in Gen 22:12). One day, in preparing for a class on Job, it occurred to me to wonder if God is ever the subject of the verb "to trust." And to my delighted amazement I found two such passages. The first occurs in Job 4:17-19, on the lips of Job's friend Eliphaz:

> Can mortal man be righteous before God?
> Can a man be pure before his Maker?
> Even in his servants *he puts no trust* [*lō' ya'ămîn*],
> and his angels he charges with error;
> how much more those who dwell in houses of clay,
> whose foundation is in the dust, who are crushed before the moth.

The second passage, likewise on Eliphaz's lips, occurs in Job 15:14-16:

> What is man, that he can be clean?
> Or he that is born of a woman, that he can be righteous?
> Behold, God *puts no trust* [*lō' ya'ămîn*] in his holy ones,
> and the heavens are not clean in his sight;
> how much less one who is abominable and corrupt,
> a man who drinks iniquity like water!

The picture that Eliphaz paints is of God as divine cosmic ruler, governing the vast universe with the help of heavenly servants and messengers. But even these heavenly beings, whom humans take to be holy, are not fully trusted in God's eyes. So God must rule by fear induced by divine might — and by suspicion embodied in the Satan. As Bildad puts Eliphaz's argument — no longer bothering to address the issue of trust (25:2-6) —

> Dominion and fear are with God;
> he makes peace in his high heaven.
> Is there any number to his armies?
> Upon whom does his light not arise?

How then can man be righteous before God?
How can he who is born of woman be clean?
Behold, even the moon is not bright
and the stars are not clean in his sight;
how much less man, who is a maggot,
and the son of man, who is a worm!

Where do Eliphaz and Bildad get this notion that God puts no trust in any person? In Num 12:7 God says of Moses, "*he is entrusted* [*neʼĕmān*] with all my house." In 1 Sam 2:35 God says, "I will raise up for myself a *faithful* [*neʼĕmān*, trustworthy] priest, who shall do according to what is in my heart and in my mind." In Neh 9:8 Ezra prays, "You found [Abraham's] heart *faithful* [*neʼĕmān*] before you." In these passages God is clearly presented as entrusting divine affairs into the hands of humans. The case of Moses in Numbers 12 is particularly suggestive. In the preceding chapter the people show their fickleness in grumbling over the manna they are given to eat and complaining that they do not have meat or vegetables such as they had enjoyed in Egypt. When Moses hears their complaining and weeping, he himself complains to God:

> Why hast thou dealt ill with thy servant? And why have I not found favor in thy sight, that thou dost lay the burden of all this people upon me? Did I conceive all this people? Did I bring them forth, that thou shouldst say to me, "Carry them in your bosom, as a nurse [*ʼōmēn*] carries the sucking child, to the land which thou didst swear to give their fathers?" Where am I to get meat to give to all this people? For they weep before me and say, "Give us meat, that we may eat." I am not able to carry all this people alone, the burden is too heavy for me. If thou wilt deal thus with me, kill me at once, if I find favor in thy sight, that I may not see my wretchedness. (Num 11:11-15)

Several things are noteworthy about this prayer. First of all, Moses portrays himself as Israel's hypothetical mother-provider, conceiving them, giving birth to them, and now carrying them as an *ʼōmēn* — a nurse, a reliable provider, one to whom the care of breast-feeding infants can be entrusted. Granted, this self-portrayal is offered protestingly. But I suspect that he is not so much refusing the role as challenging God to live up to the role of divine giver of conception and birth and nurture — the divine role summed up, as we have seen, in Gen 49:25. (We may compare also Deut 32:18, following 32:10-14.) That Moses is in fact protesting to God *on behalf of* this people is suggested in his desperate question (recognizable to any mother with no money to buy food for her clamoring children), "Where am I to get meat to give to all these people?" The second thing to notice is the boldness with which Moses challenges God. If Moses is God's servant entrusted with all God's house (Num 12:7), his faithful trusteeship apparently does not rule out such challenges. Indeed, we may view the intercessory scenes in Exodus 32 and Numbers 14, where Moses challenges God's threat against the covenant community and pleads on its behalf, as further examples of his faithful exercise of the stewardship God has entrusted to him.

So where do Eliphaz and Bildad get the idea that God trusts no one? The implied model of divine-human relations, especially as Bildad paints it in Job 25, is royal-political. It is a model that, when taken to extremes and leached of the ethos of kinship, leaves no room for trust and generosity, but reduces all interactions to the level of strictly equivalent exchange undergirded by the threat of force. All that is missing from such a picture is the figure of the Satan who, because the heavenly and the earthly members of the divine realm cannot be trusted, must travel here and there throughout the realm like Scanlon, looking all the more for evidence of corruption.

I take Eliphaz's explicit denials as the unwitting foil for what we see to the contrary in the Prologue. The glory hidden in Job's trial consists in this: that he, as God's servant, is entrusted with the task of vindicating both himself and God from the Satan's accusations — the task of vindicating the terrible yet glorious drama of life as the inexhaustible mystery of reciprocal generosity and mutual trust, persisting through inexplicable suffering and finally vindicated in the face of all attempts to reduce it to the deadening operations of a calculator.

Job's Friends

Since we all know from Job 1:8 and 2:3 what God thinks of Job, and since we all know from Job 42:7 what God thinks of the friends, we all know that they are the "heavies" in this story. Indeed, since they increasingly and falsely accuse Job of wrongdoing, they may even be taken as unwitting instruments of the Satan of the Prologue. To put this another way, as they speak in the name of their religion and out of their understanding of God, they may be taken as representing the demonic potential that lurks within any intense religious conviction, however sincerely that conviction is held. The saying that "even the Devil can quote Scripture" (see Matt 4:6) will be amply if implicitly exemplified in the friends' mounting charges against Job.

Because we know that the friends are false accusers, and that the book of Job offers a stinging critique of theologies of strict reward and punishment, it is easy for us to dismiss everything they say as wrong. It is easy to identify only with Job the wrongly accused and in sympathy with him to resist — and in our own minds shout down — what the friends have to say in the name of their religious understanding. But that is a mistake.

For one thing, the friends speak for us. If we are honest with ourselves, we will acknowledge that we have often interpreted our experience or (more likely) someone else's with some version of the theology of "just deserts," as when we say or think "they had it coming" or "what goes around comes around." If we have not formulated such a theology with their degree of stridency, it may be because we have not found ourselves involved in as intense and prolonged debate as they.

Moreover, our sympathy for Job should require us to listen with some sympathy to the arguments of the friends. For Job himself shares their theology. As the debate goes on, Job several times resorts to the imagery of a court of law, and within such a setting not only asserts his innocence but asserts God's injustice for treating him other than he deserves. The difference between Job and his friends is not a difference in their respective theologies. The difference lies in the fact that they conclude from the theology that Job is wicked and deserved what he is suffering, while he, maintaining his innocence, concludes that God is unjust and capricious in dealing with humankind.

And if Job's friends were simply and totally wrong — if there is no sense in which justice operates in the world — the only sane response on our part should be to go mad. The natural sciences operate on the assumption that the operations of the physical universe "make sense," that causes lead to effects, and that a given set of causes will always lead to a given set of effects. This is the theoretical assumption that underlies all controlled experiments. We operate with a more informal version of the same assumption in our daily lives. For example, we play soccer with an inflated ball. We do not use a granite rock of the same size; for it would not fly through the air when we kick it, and we would break our toes in the attempt. When we salt our food, it does not turn sweet; when we put sugar on our cereal it does not turn sour. If the physical universe began to behave in a totally erratic and unpredictable way we would go out of our minds, or at least curl up in a corner fearful of venturing out into it. I remember reading of an experiment with rats. As the experiment began, rats were trained to press a blue button in order to obtain a morsel of food. Their training was reinforced by the fact that when they pressed a nearby red button they received an unpleasant shock. Once they had learned the significance of these two buttons, the significance of the buttons was randomized. No longer did the blue button always give food, nor the red button always give a shock. On any given attempt, there was no way for the rats to know whether they would get food or a shock. The rats suffered a nervous breakdown.

Good parents — what the British psychoanalyst D. W. Winnicott calls "good enough" parents — know that while there may be a variety of acceptable styles of parenting, a given parent needs to be consistent in his or her dealings with a child. Conversely, the child needs to learn that certain kinds of behavior typically lead to certain kinds of results and that successful and rewarding human interactions depend on mutual recognition of this fact. There is ample room, within reciprocally generous and mutually trusting relationships, for novelty and surprise. And where the surprises are unpleasant, arising through innocent error or human moral imperfection, the fund of trusting generosity can generate freedom for forgiveness and apology. But where the choreography of human relations breaks down and parties become deaf to the music, moving in merely random and capricious ways, chaos ensues and relationship becomes impossible.

The friends' mistake was not that they believed in the principle of cause and effect, but that they came to articulate it with increasing rigidity. One sign of the rigidity with which they held it was their belief that in the case of human suffering one can always confidently infer its moral and religious cause. But this is not always possible even in today's highly developed medical world. Symptoms are effects. Some symptoms may have only one possible set of causes. But often, a given set of symptoms is consistent with a variety of causes. For example, certain kinds of pain in the chest are consistent with simple angina, involving no damage to the heart, and with an actual heart attack resulting in cardiac damage, as well as "heartburn" or acid reflux owing to an esophageal hernia. Analogously, there are many instances where suffering is a symptom of one's own wrongdoing. When people die from cirrhosis of the liver after prolonged abuse of alcohol, they can be said to "bring it on themselves." When one disregards signs to slow down for a sharp turn ahead and crashes into a concrete bridge abutment, the results are that person's own responsibility. The conviction of Job's friends that unethical behavior leads to ruin is not without widespread verification in human experience. Alfred North Whitehead put the matter this way: "The instability of evil is the moral order in the world."[5] Houses built on sand will not withstand a category five hurricane, but houses built on rock will stand a better chance.

The Beginning of the Debate

It is important to notice how Job's friend Eliphaz first voices his conviction as to "the moral order in the world." He offers it diffidently, sympathetically, and supportively, and then only after his seven-day silence in identification with Job is broken by Job's outburst in ch. 3.

> If one ventures a word with you, will you be offended? (4:2)

How gentle!

> Is not your fear of God your confidence,
> and the integrity of your ways your hope?
> Think now, who that was innocent ever perished?
> Or where were the upright cut off? (4:6-7)

Eliphaz first affirms Job's character and then encourages him to place his hope in the moral order in the world. In doing so he offers to Job what Job himself had offered to others in their times of trouble (4:3-4).

But he soon slips from encouraging Job on the basis of his character to painting a vivid picture of the other side of that theology, the trouble that the wicked sow and then themselves reap. How is that supposed to help Job? To a tender conscience wracked in grief, may it not come across as an implied hint of accusation? Worse is yet to come. Eliphaz now moves to a

---

5. Alfred North Whitehead, *Religion in the Making.* Lowell Lectures, 1926 (rev. ed. New York: Fordham University Press, 1996) 95.

perspective within which the difference between upright and wicked people becomes insignificant, for universal human imperfection leaves all alike liable to trouble and suffering (4:12-18). In fact, he concludes bleakly,

> Human beings are born to trouble
> just as sparks fly upward. (5:7)

But Eliphaz then backs away and reverts to his earlier theme — that God will punish the wicked and save the poor and needy (5:8-16). Then he encourages Job to view his suffering as part of the divine pedagogy:

> Happy is the one whom God reproves [hōkîaḥ];
> therefore do not despise the discipline [mûsār] of Shadday. (5:17)

This discipline may be painful; but if Job will only submit to it he will eventually be restored to well-being and prosperity (5:18-27).

Let us reflect for a moment on two of the words in 5:17. The verb hōkîaḥ means, basically, "to weigh" and "assess" someone else's actions for their appropriateness and either approve or disapprove of them. The noun mûsār, like its cognate verb yissar, refers to actions taken to correct another's moral behavior. This noun and its cognate verb occur frequently in reference to the relations between parent and child. Proverbs 3:11-12 provides an instructive example:

> My son, do not despise the Lord's discipline [mûsār]
> or be weary of his reproof [tōkaḥat],
> for the Lord reproves [yōkîah] him whom he loves,
> as a father the son in whom he delights.

As this text shows, these two words are at home in the sphere of parent-child pedagogy and arise in a context of positive parental concern — indeed, love and delight — for the child.

In view of our study of Shadday in the ancestral narratives of Genesis, we should not be surprised that this name for God enters the dialogue precisely at this point where Eliphaz interprets Job's sufferings as part of the divine pedagogy. If his earlier reasoning in 4:2–5:16 could be construed in more impersonal terms, as the outworking of intrinsic cause-and-effect or of august divine judgment, here he concludes on a gentler note, implicitly presenting God in parental terms. One wonders if he attempts in this way to connect up with "where Job is" in his grief — an existential "location" that is vividly identified in Job's outburst in ch. 3.

That outburst takes the form of a curse on the day of Job's birth and the night of his conception (3:3-10). What was the point of his birth, and what was the point or significance of his nurture as an infant (3:11-12), if the outcome of it all was to find himself in misery and in bitterness of soul (3:20)? The God of whom the Satan had spoken as "hedging" Job in with blessings of prosperity (1:10) Job now experiences as "hedging" him in with suffering (3:23). In place of the nurture which God had provided starting at his mother's breast, Job now has only sighing for his bread and groaning for his drink (3:24; cf. Ps 42:3).

When, then, Eliphaz attempts to encourage Job by counseling him to submit to Shaddai as a caring divine parent concerned only with his moral improvement, Job finds this counsel so much loathsome food, tasteless and unpalatable (6:5-7). So extreme are his sufferings that he cannot imagine any parent, human or divine, subjecting a child to such extreme measures. Instead, he now experiences Shaddai as an enemy attacking him with poison arrows (6:4). In the face of such an attack (see also 7:12, 20), he loses hope, loses heart, and longs to die (6:8-13). The spectacle of human life now appears to him, on the one hand, as one long, drawn-out piece of slave labor without any wages (7:1-5) and, on the other hand, as a quickly woven thread whose hopeless end comes all too soon (7:6; the Hebrew is a pun on homonyms meaning "thread" and "hope," both *tiqwâ*).

Bildad immediately leaps to God's defense: "Does God pervert justice? Does Shaddai pervert the right?" (8:3) Acknowledging that Job's sufferings need not indicate his own wickedness, Bildad poses the possibility that his children have perished for their own transgression (8:4). So Bildad takes up the theme of Eliphaz's concluding words and counsels Job to "seek God and make supplication to Shaddai" (8:5), who will surely restore him to a state of well-being even greater than he had previously known (8:6-7).

From here on what began as a pastoral visit to a suffering friend degenerates into a theological argument, in which both sides become locked by their own stubbornness into the same paradigm of reward and punishment, a paradigm which moves Job at several points to resort to the imagery of a court of law and to accusations of God as an unjust judge whose so-called wisdom is in the service of savage and sadistic displays of overwhelming power.

The Impossible Triangle

We may note, at this point, how the logic of this reward-punishment paradigm is presented in modern-day discussions of Joban suffering. Again and again, we come across what I call the impossible triangle. We are to picture a triangle, each point of which supports a theological proposition: (1) God is all-powerful; (2) God is all-good; (3) Innocent people suffer through no fault of their own. One can find a version of this impossible triangle in Harold Kushner's popular book, *When Bad Things Happen to Good People.*[6] However, many who have written on human suffering draw attention to its impossibility. What is impossible about this triangle is that one supposedly cannot affirm all three propositions at once. That is logically impossible. One may consistently affirm any two of them, but a third will have to be given up. As points on a single logical grid the three are incompatible.

For one resolution of the logical problem we may turn to Ann Conrad Lammers, who wrote a study of the intellectual collaboration between Carl Gustav Jung and the Roman Catholic theologian Victor White. Their collaboration was mutually enriching and satisfying until Jung published his book, *Answer to Job.*[7] At that point the two men became estranged over Jung's assertion that God is not unambiguously good. Only when White entered the last stages of terminal cancer did the two men become reconciled. Lammers summarizes Jung's views this way:

> As one compelled to wrestle naked with an interior God of absolute power and only relative moral trustworthiness, Jung bore a superhuman burden. For he felt himself called as a mere mortal to reach into the shadows and relieve the sorrows of the world, while remaining staunchly unwilling to rely on a God of ultimate goodness or to accept the sacramental mediation of a corporately attested faith.
>
> Based on Job's experience, God is discovered [for Jung] to be not a "good" personal being, but a *complexio oppositorum.* Human beings know enough about goodness and justice so that they could recognize absolute transcendent goodness if they saw it. . . . But God (or the God-image) should not be called *summum Bonum.* . . . [T]o ascribe unmixed

6. (New York: Schocken, 1981).
7. (1952; Eng. trans. London: Routledge & Paul, 1954).

60

goodness and justice to God is an insult to human suffering and over-loads humanity with undeserved blame.[8]

In contrast to Jung, who opted for propositions (1) and (3) and was unable to hold on to (2), Harold Kushner held on to propositions (2) and (3) and, by the logic of the impossible triangle, was obliged — in spite of the testimony of his tradition's Scriptures — to relinquish (1). As we have seen, Job's friends, convinced of propositions (1) and (2), were driven to deny proposition (3) and conclude that Job's sufferings were evidence of his guilt and so were deserved.

The Dilemma, or Rather, Trilemma

But if it is impossible to make all three affirmations at once, all three of these two-proposition solutions, involving as they do the denial of a third, raise grave problems for religious sensibility. To say that all suffering is the deserved result of the sufferer's own wrongdoing is to add insult to injury and to add grievously to the suffering. This "blames the victim," attacking the victim's conscience (cf. Job in 27:6) and isolating him or her in it (like Job in ch. 19). Or worse yet, this violates that conscience by persuading it to take on a burden of false guilt. It is remarkable how often the psalms present us with a cry to God for vindication against false accusers, and how often that cry arises as the voice of one who feels alone and bereft of supporting witnesses. (Psalm 12 is a good example; and we may compare Job's cry in 16:18, "O earth, cover not my blood, and let my cry find no resting place.") If we would hold that God is both all-powerful and all-good, we dare not do so at the cost of silencing such cries.

The claim that "human beings know enough about goodness and justice so that they could recognize absolute transcendent goodness if they saw it" raises complex and, indeed, perplexing issues. When Jesus says to his disciples, "I have food to eat of which you do not know" (John 4:32), he speaks of something they do not know; and yet it is like something they know. If they, like any human being, know what it is to hunger and what it is to eat and be satisfied, then in some sense they know what he is talking

8. Ann Conrad Lammers, *In God's Shadow: The Collaboration of Victor White and C. G. Jung* (New York: Paulist, 1994) 152, 190.

about. But that knowledge does not by itself provide them with the basis of recognizing fully what he is talking about. Really to know what Jesus is talking about calls for being able to say, with all the range and depth and unreserved self-spending with which he says it, "my food is to do the will of him who sent me and to accomplish his work" (John 4:34). So too with justice and goodness. We know something of these principles, these ideals. And what we know of them is terribly important. But does that knowledge necessarily enable us to recognize absolute transcendent goodness when confronted with it? Like Jung's light of consciousness (which I shall come to in a moment), we must not relinquish the knowledge we have of justice and goodness. Yet it seems to me that modesty requires us to be prepared to acknowledge that such knowledge is but a broken reflection of the justice and the goodness at the heart of God.

The problem with Jung's statement, and with all arguments from the triangle that give up on divine goodness or justice, is that in doing so we pay ourselves the compliment of possessing within ourselves the high-water mark of moral consciousness. That is a claim on behalf of the human race, or even on behalf of the finest moral consciousnesses among us, which I for one find immodest. The implication is that in this respect we are superior to God and in a position to instruct God on issues of right and wrong. But then, who among us is to be the teacher? Especially now, in our so-called postmodern world, there will be many applicants for the position, and not only their credentials but their pedagogical programs will differ from one another. And if our claim to possess a moral consciousness superior to God's in fact amounts to self-deification (as in Gen 3:5, "you will be like God [or "gods"], knowing good and evil"), the result will be a cacophonous polytheism.

The dilemma posed by the issues in the preceding paragraph is not easily resolved. We may pose it as the dilemma of conscience. In his memoir, *Memories, Dreams, Reflections,* Jung gives powerful and poignant expression to the centrality of consciousness. The passage deserves to be quoted in full:

> About this time I had a dream which both frightened and encouraged me. It was night in some unknown place, and I was making slow and painful headway against a mighty wind. Dense fog was flying along everywhere. I had my hands cupped around a tiny light which threatened to go out at any moment. Everything depended on my keeping this little

light alive. Suddenly I had the feeling that something was coming up behind me. I looked back, and saw a gigantic black figure following me. But at the same moment I was conscious, in spite of my terror, that I must keep my little light going through night and wind, regardless of all dangers. When I awoke, I realized at once that the figure was a "specter of the Brocken," my own shadow on the swirling mists, brought into being by the little light I was carrying. I knew, too, that this little light was my consciousness, the only light I have. My own understanding is the sole treasure I possess, and the greatest. Though infinitely small and fragile, in comparison with the powers of darkness, it is still a light, my only light.[9]

To this, Job surely would utter a vehement "amen." If the proverb can say "the human spirit [*něšāmâ*] is the lamp of the Lord, searching every innermost part" (Prov 20:27), Job, when he finally swears an oath of innocence, in 27:2-6, can say,

> as long as my breath [*něšāmâ*] is in me,
> and the spirit [*rûaḥ*] of God is in my nostrils, . . .
> I will hold fast my righteousness, and will not let it go;
> my heart does not reproach me for any of my days.

But is the light that is in Job, or Jung, or any of us, the brightest of lights? It may be the only light we have; and however small, in comparison with the powers of darkness it is still a light. But in comparison with the light of God, is it brighter? Paul will write to the Corinthian church, "I am not aware of anything against myself, but I am not thereby acquitted. It is the Lord who judges me" (1 Cor 4:4). The struggle in which we are all engaged, it seems to me, is to live by the light we have and to guard that light with all the care that Jung so vividly urges, while yet remaining open to further light even if that light discloses shadows within our depths. As we shall see, Job's oath enacts this kind of openness and is pivotal in the outcome to his story.

What then of proposition (1), that God is all-powerful? Shall we abandon it? But how can we? If we abandon this proposition, we face the prospect that, for some of us at least, Job's words in 7:6 are the final truth: "My

9. C. G. Jung, *Memories, Dreams, and Reflections* (New York: Vintage, 1963) 87-88.

days are swifter than a weaver's shuttle, and come to their end without *tiqwâ.*" The garment of our life, begun on the divine loom in such hope (*tiqwâ*), according to some design and for some purpose, must be left unfinished because the divine weaver has run out of thread (*tiqwâ*). God whose goodness is manifest in other lives that have come to a beautiful rounded conclusion does not possess the resources to bring my life, or someone else's life, to such a place, but must leave its loose ends dangling.

In such a view, God cannot "comprehend at once" all that is necessary to the completion of the divine purpose in some lives, and so, in a divine version of "Sophie's Choice,"[10] must drop some packages in order to hold on to others. I find that prospect unbearable. I remember, as a child during World War II, waking from a nightmare in which my hometown was overrun by enemy forces who took our whole family captive. At one point, it was decided that one of our family would have to be put to death, so our captors turned to me and insisted that I name the candidate for execution. In the dream I could not bear to let go of any of the others, so volunteered myself. I hasten to add that the dream no doubt showed me to myself as I would like to think of myself, and it would remain a dubious question as to whether I would live up to that ideal in an actual crisis. But it illustrates the dilemma: How can any one life be "complete" when other lives are left dangling like loose threads? In that case, if a good God is not all-powerful — by which I would mean, if a good God is not capable of bringing the divine design for creation to successful completion — the whole human, the whole cosmic, story is in danger of unraveling from its loose threads and so is without hope.

The value of the "impossible triangle," it seems to me, lies in its identification of the "trilemma" faced by the person in Frost's poem: The triangle identifies with stark clarity the extremes we find too hard to comprehend at once. But each point on the triangle identifies something we dare not leave behind. This means that we must drop the load and try to restack it. One problem with the triangle as typically discussed is that it embodies an attempt to hold the issues simply "with hand and mind." In the first instance, we look around us for actions on the human plane that embody unambiguous power and unambiguous goodness while recognizing the plight of the truly innocent. Instead, we too often witness enactments of power that ride roughshod over the innocent and thereby display their

(see page 2)

10. William Styron, *Sophie's Choice* (New York: Random House, 1979).

want of goodness. Or we witness the ineffectuality of goodness to thwart the unjust enactments of brute power. Or, worst of all, we see religious dogmatists impugn the integrity of innocent sufferers in order to defend the doctrines of divine goodness and power. The temptation here is to think through the issues with the aid of unambiguous terms, of the sort exemplified by traditional logic: A is A; A is not B; and A cannot be and not be B at one and the same time. First we define all-power precisely, adequately, and unambiguously. Then we do the same with all-goodness. Then we do the same with innocence. And then we discover that the three, as separately defined, won't hold together — they are incompatible.

(paradox)

Incompatibility for Hand, Head, and Heart

But a comment on "incompatibility" by Alfred North Whitehead may help us here. Whitehead was, among other things, one of the giants of the world of mathematical logic at the turn of the nineteenth and twentieth centuries, co-authoring *Principia Mathematica* with his colleague Bertrand Russell.[11] When he came to write his philosophical masterwork, *Process and Reality: An Essay in Cosmology,* Whitehead took the concept of incompatibility with great seriousness. But at one point he characterized this "essay in cosmology" as "a critique of pure feeling." In doing so he deliberately set it over against Immanuel Kant's masterwork, *The Critique of Pure Reason.* At one point, in a chapter titled "From Descartes to Kant," Whitehead notes that "Dr. H. M. Sheffer has pointed out the fundamental logical importance of the notion of 'incompatibility.'" On the same page, he writes, "'feelings' are the entities which are primarily 'compatible' or 'incompatible.' All other usages of these terms are derivative."[12] In making this last statement, Whitehead had in mind that the word "compatible" is based on the Latin verb *pati,* "to bear, suffer." It is cognate with our word "compassion," which *Webster's New Collegiate Dictionary* defines as "sympathetic consciousness of others' distress together with a desire to alleviate it."[13]

In spelling out his understanding of how the world works, Whitehead

11. (Cambridge: Cambridge University Press, 1910).

12. Alfred North Whitehead, *Process and Reality: An Essay in Cosmology,* Gifford Lectures, 1927-28 (New York: Macmillan, 1929) 225.

13. 2nd ed. (Springfield, MA: Merriam, 1960).

coins a term which is fundamental to his exposition: "prehend." He could have used the familiar terms "apprehend" or "comprehend," except that these terms tend to make us think too quickly of intellectual operations. He wants a term that can apply to any operation in the cosmos, whether, as he puts it, "the vibrant pulsations of emotion or the vibrations of physical matter in far-off space."[14] So, he says, any occasion of experience arises by a process of "prehending" items in the world around it and making them in some way a part of itself. We become who we become by "prehending" aspects of the surrounding world into ourselves. But we prehend anything by "feeling" it — by identifying it in its own specific quality and character and accepting that quality and character into ourselves where it becomes part of our own internal constitution. But whatever we prehend, or "feel into ourselves," *itself* has arisen as *its* feeling into *itself* of aspects of its own world. So our prehending or feeling of other things is a sym-pathetic feeling, a feeling of their feelings with them. But here is where the issue of compatibility arises. Suppose we are presented with two or more factors in our environment that are marked by feelings widely or intensely at odds with each other: Can we adequately "prehend" both of these factors at the same time? Suppose a mother who has three children, each of which has its own experience and issues, and those issues lead the children to be at loggerheads with each other. So intense do their divergent and conflicting agendas become that they consider them to be incompatible. What does the mother do? With sympathetic maternal feeling she perceives how each of them feels about things. Her feeling for them may not be uncritical. Indeed, precisely because she is their mother she wishes for them not simply what they want for themselves but what is best for them. So her sympathetic feeling may be accompanied by feelings for each child that diverge from the feelings each has for itself. Moreover, as their mother she somehow has to keep the family together; and simply taking the side of one of them against the other two, or the side of two of them against a third, is unacceptable to her. Somehow, she feels, she has to find a way to "keep their building balanced at her breast." For she will not — simply will not — leave any of them behind. What does she do? Her powers of action may fail her. Her powers of reflection may fail to provide her with understand-

14. Cf. his claim that "the energetic activity considered in physics is the emotional intensity entertained in life." Alfred North Whitehead, *Modes of Thought* (New York: Macmillan, 1938) 168.

ing as to why they are behaving in mutually antagonistic ways. She finds herself unable to hold them with hand and mind. But one thing she can and will do: she will hold them with her heart. That is, if her heart can grow capacious and strong enough to be stretched in so many different directions without breaking. Sometimes, perhaps because of some personal bitterness or other hurt, her heart will give way. Sometimes, despite her most embracing maternal intentions, it simply is not strong enough. Sometimes the pain of having to let go with hand and mind — as when economic or other circumstances drive a mother to offer up her child for adoption — is too great. Sometimes the very intensity of maternal feeling in such situations is unmatched by the strength to bear it, and to survive the mother smothers her feeling or somehow mutes it. In Second Isaiah, God says to Zion,

> Can a woman forget her sucking child,
> that she should have no compassion [*raḥēm*]
> on the child of her womb?
> Even these may forget,
> yet I will not forget you.
> Behold, I have graven you
> on the palms of my hands. (Isa 49:15-16)

It may be that we are unable to "comprehend at once" the issues of divine all-power and all-goodness and of human innocence — not with our hands, not with our minds, not even with our hearts. What of God? Does God have a capacity to hold extremes that we ourselves know not of? That, it seems to me, is the testimony and hope of Psalm 131 which we considered in Chapter One.

5. Lust for Life and the Bitterness of Job

In Chapter Two, I sketched two biblical paradigms for divine-human relations, clan-personal and cosmic-political, and I associated them with the figures of Abraham and Moses. I also sketched the biblical basis for my proposal that, of these two paradigms, the Abrahamic is foundational and the Mosaic superstructural. In computer terms, the Mosaic paradigm is the "customized default position" of Israel before God, but the Abrahamic paradigm is the "original default position." The significance of this, as I attempted to show from a consideration of the golden calf crisis, is that when Israel's customized default position suffers a fatal system error, Israel's relation with God survives and continues by reversion to the original default position.

In Chapter Three, I observed that the argument between Job and his friends takes place predominantly in the context of the Mosaic paradigm. Their language concerning justice and wickedness, innocence and guilt, gravitates increasingly — especially on Job's part — toward a court of law and its proceedings. (To be sure, nowhere in Job do we find any explicit reference to the Sinai covenant and its statutes and ordinances, nor to the exodus which preceded that covenant. Of course not. Such direct references would subvert the distancing strategy that I identified in Chapter One, a strategy by which the author of Job enables the exilic and postexilic community to engage its plight before God indirectly and, as it were, at arm's length.) In such a setting, Job repeatedly views God as his unjust accuser and his unjust judge. As he complains already in Job 9, how is he to gain a fair hearing when his judge is also his accuser? But in Chapter Four, I began to identify elements of the ancestral paradigm as they are reflected in Eliphaz's introduction of the name and themes of Shadday and also in Job's opening outburst in Job 3.

In this chapter I will propose that, for all the prominence of the justice/law-court paradigm in the arguments of Job and his friends, the paradigm of clan religion is in fact primary in this book. And I will propose why, if it is primary, its themes run through Job as an undercurrent rather than as the predominant topic of their debate. Before we look into Job for signs of this undercurrent, it will be helpful to consider briefly some representative contemporary understandings of human psychosocial development. These understandings will shed additional light on the relation between foundational and subsequent patterns that give shape to human life.

A Perspective from Developmental Psychology

We may begin with the work of Erik Erikson. In two influential books, *Childhood and Society* and *Insight and Responsibility,*[1] Erikson developed a model of human development through eight successive stages of life. In his analysis, each stage is marked by a developmental task distinctive to that stage. Ideally, an individual's development proceeds by the successful completion of the task distinctive to a given stage, which then becomes a stable basis for launching into the next stage with its new developmental task. Where a previous stage was not successfully or adequately completed, it leaves that task as something still to be worked on remedially in later life. Erikson's model was picked up and correlated with religious concerns in the work of W. W. Meissner, and we may turn to his work for specific details. In his book, *Life and Faith: Psychological Perspectives on Religious Experience,* Meissner presents the following outline:[2]

Anyone who has witnessed an infant nursing at its mother's breast, and then sleeping quietly there or in its crib, will appreciate what Meissner and other psychoanalysts call the "oral-respiratory" phase of development, enacted in the mode of "incorporation." The infant, like all of us, is utterly dependent for its moment-to-moment existence on the air that it breathes. It is similarly dependent on the regular intake of its mother's milk or other

---

1. Erik H. Erikson, *Childhood and Society* (New York: Norton, 1950); *Insight and Responsibility* (New York: Norton, 1964).

2. (Washington: Georgetown University Press, 1987) 63.

Comparative Development of the Psychosocial and Psychospiritual Organism

Stages of Growth	Psychosexual phases	Psychosocial crises	Psychospiritual crises
Infancy	Oral-respiratory (incorporative mode)	Trust/mistrust	Faith, hope
Early childhood	Anal-urethral (retentive-eliminative mode)	Autonomy/shame, doubt	Contrition
Play age	Infantile-genital (intrusive mode)	Initiative/guilt	Penance, temperance
School age	Latency period	Industry/inferiority	Fortitude
Adolescence	Puberty (genital maturity)	Identity/identity diffusion	Humility
Young adulthood	Genitality	Intimacy/isolation	Love of neighbor
Adulthood		Generativity/self-absorption	Service, zeal, self-sacrifice
Maturity		Integrity/despair, disgust, self-contempt	Charity

means of nourishment. In the earliest days and weeks, the trust involved in the extension of its mouth to the mother's breast appears to be overwhelmingly instinctual and organic; but as the weeks pass and the pattern is repeated, that trust takes on overtones of conscious attitude; in time it can express itself in a trust that persists in the face of its mother's sudden temporary absence. That trust then turns into hope, expressing itself in crying, even angry howling, rather than the silence of mute apathy and despair.

The developmental tasks of autonomy, initiative, and responsibility, with their attendant issues of self-affirmation or shame, clear or clouded conscience, and so on, arise later. But, as Erikson has underscored, the earliest task — the development of the capacity for faith and hope — is foundational to all the others, for that developmental task is not so much superseded by the following developmental tasks, as carried forward to them. The "virtue" (if we may call it that) of elemental trust/faith is called for in each new phase, because each new phase presents aspects of the world and of the developing self that the person has not previously encountered. The "terrible two's," familiar to all parents, are terrible because during that period a child is entering upon a strange new world and must learn new skills both in interpreting it and in responding to it. Where the earlier task of trust/faith has been accomplished with a reasonable degree of success (usually in response to the reliability of the caregivers in providing for its needs), this energy of faith has a challenging enough time coping with this new world. Likewise, in each subsequent phase faith is both carried forward and relearned, along with the other skills that are being learned for the first time. (When, even after a long life that has navigated its developmental phases in exemplary fashion, one approaches the "undiscovered country" of death, one should not be surprised if one's faith is set a new task for its trust.)

According to the psychoanalytic tradition from Sigmund Freud onward, one may experience, as a key psychological dynamic, a psychodynamic movement called "regression." Confronted with issues that one cannot for the moment cope with, and overwhelmed by them — or confronted with the need to cope more effectively with issues of long ago that had been bypassed or repressed — one is said to "regress" from a later mode of psycho-social functioning to an earlier stage. The impression can be gained that such a move is unfortunate, that "we're grown up now and should be beyond all that; let's behave like adults."

Daniel N. Stern, in his book, *The Interpersonal Life of the Infant*, argues for a different way of understanding these matters. In doing so, he proposes that instead of developmental "phases" we should speak of developmental "domains," for the word "phase" emphasizes temporal sequence. As such it reinforces the view that

> the infant's world view shifts dramatically as each new stage is ushered in, and the world is seen dominantly, if not exclusively, in terms of the organization of the new stage. What happens, then, to the previous phases, to the earlier world views? Either they are eclipsed and drop out or . . . they remain dormant but become integrated into the emergent organization and thereby lose much of their previous character.[3]

Stern pictures this understanding of development in the following way:

3. (New York: Basic Books, 1985) 29.

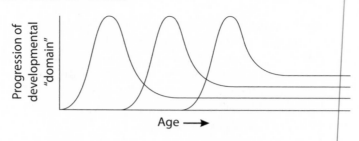

In such an understanding, "regression" to earlier phases occurs only under special conditions of "challenge, stress, conflict, failure of adaptation, or fatigue, and in dream states, psychopathological conditions, or drug states." In regression the person is viewed as being pulled *back* "in developmental time, to experience the world in a manner similar to the way it was experienced earlier." But "with the exception of these regressions, developing world views are mainly successive and sequential, not simultaneous." (I propose that we may correlate Stern's language about "world views" with my language about "default settings" and "paradigms.")

Stern's research into infant development leads him to propose a different model, in which the infant's development proceeds not so much by displacement or supersession (my terms) but by augmentation. He pictures this development as indicated in the diagram on page 72. He writes:

> All domains of relatedness remain active during development. The infant does not grow out of any of them; none of them atrophy, none become developmentally obsolete or get left behind. And once all domains are available, there is no assurance that any one domain will necessarily claim preponderance during any particular age period. None has a privileged status all of the time. Since there is an orderly temporal succession of emergence of each domain during development . . . there will inevitably be periods when one or two domains hold predominance by default[!]. In fact, each successive organizing subjective perspective requires the preceding one as a precursor. *Once formed, the domains remain forever as distinct forms of experiencing social life and self.* It is for this reason that the term *domains* of relatedness has been chosen, rather than *phases* or *stages.*[4]

4. Stern, *The Interpersonal Life of the Infant,* 32-33 (first italics added).

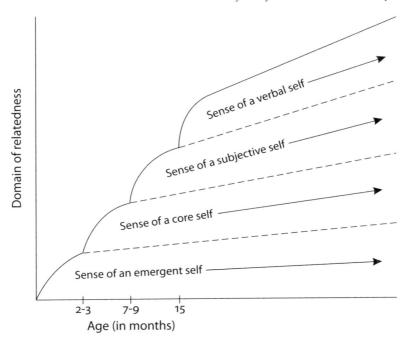

An image that I have found helpful is to think of making a stringed instrument, in which one installs first one string, and then another, and then another. With the first string, one can already play a simple tune by "stopping" it with a finger to vary its vibrating length and thereby its tune. With the second string, one can now play either a simple tune on it or a more complex tune involving both strings. With each new string the combination of possibilities multiplies. But any earlier string, once installed, remains as contemporary as any of the others, and is as available for music as any later string. As Stern sums up,

> While these domains of relatedness result in qualitative shifts in social experience, they are not phases; rather, they are forms of social experience that remain intact throughout life. . . . Subjective social experience results from the sum and integration of experience in all domains.[5]

5. Stern, *The Interpersonal Life of the Infant*, 34.

If we may combine the work of Erikson and Meissner with that of Stern, we may say that the first "domain" to arise enjoys a foundational status that makes it unique, throughout life, among the other domains. What others have called "regression" is then not simply a move from one domain among other equal domains; it is a move to that domain which remains primal — it is a return to home base. This is borne out by the research of John Bowlby and his associates, summed up in his book from which I quoted in Chapter Three. It will be helpful to have that quotation before us again:

> An ordinary devoted mother provides a child with a secure base from which he can explore and to which he can return when upset or frightened. . . . This concept, of the secure personal base, from which a child, an adolescent, or an adult goes out to explore and to which he returns from time to time, is one I have come to regard as crucial for an understanding of how an emotionally stable person develops and functions *all through his life.*[6]

And what is the significance of this "secure personal base"? For the answer to that, we may listen again to the exchange between Frost's farming couple:

> "Home is the place where, when you have to go there,
> They have to take you in."
>   "I should have called it
> Something you somehow haven't to deserve."[7]

The Case of Job

Let us now take note of the "domain" within which Job breaks into anguished speech in ch. 3. It is the domain of conception, gestation, birth, and first nurture at the breast:

> Let the day perish wherein I was born,
> and the night which said, "A man-child is conceived." . . .

6. John Bowlby, *A Secure Base: Parent-Child Attachment and Healthy Human Development* (New York: Basic Books, 1988) 46.
7. *Collected Poems, Prose, & Plays* (New York: Library of America, 1995) 43.

Why did I not die at birth,
come forth from the womb and expire?
Why did the knees receive me?
Or why the breasts, that I should suck? . . .
Why is light given to him that is in misery,
and life to *the bitter in soul?* (3:3, 11-12, 20)

This is the same domain we see him speaking out of in response to the first set of calamities in ch. 1:

Naked I came from my mother's womb,
and naked shall I return;
The Lord gave, and the Lord has taken away;
blessed be the name of the Lord. (1:21)

In this first shock, Job had responded, as it were, on automatic pilot. Having lived a life of blessing and prosperity, hitherto protected ("hedged") from danger, he had learned in each new stage how to enact, in modes appropriate to that stage, the first lessons of trust learned in his mother's womb and at her breast. Now, his senses and his understanding mercifully narcotized by the numbness of shock, the primal response of trust to which his long life had habituated him took over. But after the second shock, and in the following seven days of silence, that numbness began to give way, and that unquestioning trust began to press toward questions, until finally his trust — if we may call it that — takes the form of a howl of bitterness at what his life has become. English translations of 3:12 typically read, "Why [*maddûaʿ*] did the knees receive me? Or why [*mâ*] the breasts, that I should suck?" But there is a shift in the Hebrew interrogative pronouns here that I believe is obscured in such translations. The primary meaning of *ma* is "what?" As one lexicon puts it, *mâ* "is often used in questions to which the answer *little,* or *nothing,* is expected, and it thus becomes equivalent to a *rhetorical negative.*"[8] "*What* is the breast . . . ?" An infant instinctively expects the breast to hold something good, something sweet and nourishing, for it. The sense of life that informs this domain of experience, when all goes well, is then a sense of life's sweetness and de-

---

8. *A Hebrew and English Lexicon of the Old Testament,* ed. Francis Brown, S. R. Driver, and Charles A. Briggs (Oxford: Clarendon, 1953) 553.

pendable goodness. But now Job's life has become filled with misery, and its taste one of bitterness. *Why* is light and life given to such a one? And even more deeply, *what* is the breast, that one should trust it in the first place only to find that that trust was betrayed. For in the paradigm of clan religion, behind the human mother's breast stands the breast of God. (We may recall the image in Isa 66:10-13 and the image in Psalm 131.) In the momentary move from *why?* to *what?* Job here briefly touches on a question deeper than God's purposes for Job; he touches on the question of the character of God.

The phrase "one bitter in soul" announces a theme that runs throughout Job's anguished speeches. Indeed, I have come to view it as announcing the central issue in Job's plight, so it will be worthwhile to consider it more closely. The Hebrew expression is "bitter in *nepeš*." This word *nepeš* has a revealing range of meaning. Physiologically, it refers to the throat, and there are a few passages in the Hebrew Bible where it displays this meaning. In the earliest form of Sumerian writing adopted by the Babylonians, the pictogram for their word *napištu* is the outline of a human head with hash marks on the throat to indicate what part of the human anatomy *napištu* names. Not surprisingly, then, *nepeš* (pronounced "nephesh") can also mean "breath," for when we breathe in the invisible air the place where we feel it is in the throat; and in any case, we can die if someone chokes off our breathing there. So again, in virtue of the life-sustaining significance of our breathing, and the relation between our breathing and the continuing well-being of our throat, *nepeš* can mean "life" or "self." But *nepeš* can also carry the meaning "appetite" and, from there, "morale, will to go on." There was a day, decades ago, when Eileen faced a pile of ironing on an oppressively hot and humid day and must have voiced some muttered mood of impossibility. Holly, who was not quite four at the time, sprang up and proposed, brightly, "Mommy, why don't you go into the family room and turn on the TV and watch 'The Edge of Night'? I can do the ironing — I have the energy, the breath, and the appetite!" She was saying that she had the *nepeš*.

We may fill out this picture by considering how the word *nepeš* works in the Garden Story in Genesis 2–3. There, God takes a clod of dust from the ground ['*ǎdāmâ*], shapes it, breathes into it the breath [*něšāmâ*] of life, and the human being, the '*ādām* that is thus created from the '*ǎdāmâ*, becomes a living *nepeš*. A living *being* (as in RSV, NRSV, NIV)? But the word "being" is too abstract and dry a term to catch the richness of *nepeš* here. A living *soul* (as in KJV)? But that is too ethereal, too exclusively spiritual. The fact that the *'ādām* (the lump of ground, or "earthling") becomes a living *nepeš* because God breathed into it the breath of life suggests that we should let the word *nepeš* resonate in all its fullness of connotation. Consider, then, how this act of creation is followed by God planting a garden with all manner of trees in it, trees luscious in appearance and good in the eating. ("Pleasant" to look at is inexcusably tepid as a translation. The adjective *neḥmād* here occurs again in Gen 3:6, where it is translated "a delight." The word is from the verb *ḥāmad,* which means "to covet, to lust after," as in Exod 20:17, and in Job 20:20-21, where it refers to appetite.) I suggest that the picture of "newborn" humankind in a garden of luscious and delightful foods, in Genesis 2, is analogous to the picture of a newborn infant in the bosom of its nursing mother. Like the earth to the humans on it, the mother is a "fruitful tree" to the infant at her breast, her milk sweet (Hebrew *nōʿam,* from which the name *noʿŏmî,* "Naomi") to the infant's taste.

But in addition to all these appetite-arousing trees, God also plants two other trees: the tree of life and the tree of the knowledge of good and evil. What does this mean? What is meant by the tree of life? Do not the other trees already serve to keep alive those who eat them? Or does the tree of life serve an appetite that is not exhausted in eating of those other trees? Does an appetite for the tree of life desire something that the appetite for those other trees (to echo Jesus in John 4) "knows not of"? What is that something? It is "life," yet not simply life as a biological function sustained by eating physical food. And what of the tree of the knowledge of good and evil? Does that entice an appetite for something that neither the tree of life nor the other trees will satisfy? We see, then, that if to be an *'ādām* is to be a living *nepeš* — a living appetite — that appetite has many dimensions, some of which are physical-biological, but some of which have to do with what we may call moral and spiritual aspects of reality. When God places the *'ādām* in this garden, God says,

> You may freely eat of every tree of the garden;
> but of the tree of the knowledge of good and evil you shall not eat,
> for in the day that you eat of it you shall die. (Gen 2:16-17)

What does this mean? It means at least this: that we are invited and encouraged, as living appetites, freely to enjoy the world that God has created, in all its capacity to sustain and delight us. But there is one tree that we are warned not to eat of. It has to do with a kind of knowledge that is reserved only to God. In the context of the present essay, I propose that we think of the tree of the knowledge of good and evil as the temptation to grasp and possess the world "with hand and mind" in such a fashion as to be able unilaterally to secure and assure our continued well-being and, in so doing, by our own efforts to make "life" our own possession. Further, it is the desire to determine and decide for ourselves what shall be called good and what shall be called evil. Why is the other odd tree, the tree of life, not even mentioned in God's address to the 'ādām? I suggest that it is because it is in trusting in the wisdom of God's prohibition, and in going ahead to eat of all the other trees *except* for the forbidden tree, that we "stumble upon" and discover ourselves to be eating the tree of life. For if all the ordinary trees in the garden go to support our biological life (good for food) and to awaken us to the aesthetic life of our senses (luscious, delightful to look at), the act of trusting obedience places us in a relationship with God in which we reciprocate the trust God placed in us in placing the tree of knowledge within our reach and then asking us not to eat it. The experience — the taste — of this mutual trust is unique. It has its closest analogy in the mutual trust that can mark the relationship between persons. But it remains unique.

I suggest that it is in enjoying this relationship of mutual trust between us and God that we eat of the tree of life. It is a food, a taste, that the suspicious, calculating, knowledge-mongering Scanlons and Satans of this world know not of. True life is not to be found in such unilateral grasping after knowledge and manipulation of the world on its basis. It is to be discovered and enjoyed in the process of entering into a relation of mutual trust with God. Such a relation does not rule out our pursuit of knowledge and understanding of how things work; but it places that pursuit within a more fundamental, and ongoing, relational context. The "frames of reference" which we develop and within which we live as a result of such pursuit of knowledge become subsequent domains of experience and relation, "customized default positions." The relation of mutual trust provides the primal position that undergirds them and to which we may and must return, as and when we "screw up" within our customized settings. For it seems to be built into the nature of things that, if we eat long enough at the tree of the knowledge of good and evil, in too narrow a preoccupation with it, eventually its fruits will sour in our mouths and will spoil our taste for even the ordinary trees. Then we become jaded, blasé, cynical, and world-weary. Then our hope lies in having our appetite for life renewed through some experience of the grace of generous trust, in some relationship or other, and through this, our appetite for the ordinaries around us.

But if a life of dissolute or grasping wickedness can turn sour in one's stomach (like the insatiably greedy person Zophar so graphically portrays in Job 20), one's appetite for life can also be dampened in quite another way — not through one's own wicked actions, but through one's own innocent calamities and griefs. This can happen in mild form, as when Holly's little brother Daniel momentarily lost his will to skate. But it can happen with grave intensity, as in the case of Job. We encounter the resulting loss of appetite for life at a number of points in his speeches. In the previous chapter I already discussed his words in 6:4-7. This loss of appetite leads immediately to his wish that he might die (6:8-9):

> O that I might have my request,
> and that God would grant my desire [*tiqwâ* — "hope"!];
> that it would please God to crush me,
> that he would let loose his hand and cut me off!

Later in this same speech, he says, "I loathe my life; I would not live forever" (7:16), and in his next speech he says again, "I loathe my life [my *nepeš*]."

One is reminded of the lines in one of Gerard Manley Hopkins's poems, "I am gall, I am heartburn, God's most deep decree/Bitter would have me taste: my taste was me."[9]

In such a state, Job says,

> What is my strength, that I should wait?
> And what is my end, that I should be patient?
> Is my strength the strength of stones,
> or is my flesh bronze?
> In truth I have no help in me,
> and any resource is driven from me. (6:11-13)

Here, the words "that I should be patient" translate a Hebrew idiom that literally means "that I should lengthen my *nepeš*." A hopeful goal or end is

---

9. *Poems of Gerard Manley Hopkins* (London: Oxford University Press, 1948) 110. The opening line of this sonnet is "I wake and feel the fell of dark, not day."

something that gives one the appetite to reach out toward it in anticipation. Indeed, it is the hope that such a goal inspires, and the appetite for it that such a goal arouses, that provides the energy and the strength to pursue that goal, or to wait for it to arrive, and while waiting to get on with life. (Is the hungry infant's indignant hungry cry, or the psalmist's frequent complaint, "How long, O Lord?" a form of pursuit or of waiting?) There is a Hebrew idiom that expresses the loss, or the dampening, of that appetite and the strength of patience it provides. That idiom means literally "to cut short the *nepeš*." The experience may be likened to having one's wind knocked out of one — having one's morale cut short. That is where Job is.

Job's Bitterness

As we have seen, the bitterness of Job's misery has called him to question the point of his birth and, implicitly, the character of the God who would bring him to this point (3:11-12, 20). In ch. 6 he describes what Shadday has now visited upon him as arrows whose poison his spirit now must drink. In the next chapter I shall trace this theme of bitterness through the book to its climax in 27:2, where Job, resuming the language of 3:20, asserts that "God has taken away my right,/and Shadday has made my *nepeš* bitter." We shall return later to Job's oath in 27:2-6. For now, we may note that an oath falls within the domain of law and its courts, while the language in the second line (along with that in v. 3) arises out of the domain of God's life-giving creativity (Gen 2:7) as instanced in Job's own case. This embedding of the domain of a courtroom proceeding within the domain of life-giving creativity occurs already in chs. 9–10. In this way the two paradigms of divine-human relation come into closest conjunction and point us to the resolution of Job's crisis. I will explore that resolution in the next two chapters.

In the meantime, we may consider the twofold nature of that crisis. That crisis, as typically identified in discussions of Job, arises over the issue of justice. Job's friends attribute his sufferings as just deserts for his sinfulness. Job views his sufferings as evidence for God's injustice toward him and in the world generally. The book of Job is often discussed as a theodicy — an attempt, as John Milton put it, to "justify the ways of God to man."[10]

10. *The Complete Poetical Works of John Milton* (Boston: Houghton Mifflin, 1965) 213 ("Paradise Lost," Book I, line 26).

But for all the importance of the issue of justice in Job, and in the Old Testament generally, it is not the only important issue, and in my view not the gravest issue. That issue is the crisis posed by the sense of God's abandonment. How can a loving God caringly bring life into the world and then cruelly abandon it to such suffering (10:8-13)? This is a question that arises again and again in the Bible.

Cries of Dereliction in the Bible

If exilic Israel can cry out in complaint that "My way is hid from the Lord,/and my right is disregarded by my God" (Isa 40:27), that same community, under the figure of Zion, later cries out, "The Lord has forsaken me,/my Lord has forgotten me" (Isa 49:14). Perhaps the most poignant cry of abandonment comes in Psalm 22, which opens,

> My God, my God, why have you forsaken me?
> Why are you so far from helping me,
> from the words of my groaning?

The sense of God's abandonment is the sense that God is far away (Ps 22:1, 11, 19), while those who are near to the psalmist are at hand not to help him but to attack him (vv. 6-8, 11-13, 16-18). What is most striking is how the psalmist appeals from that sense of abandonment to the God who was previously present and active in his life. First he makes the general affirmation (vv. 4-5 [Heb. 5-6]) that

> In you our ancestors trusted [*bāṭĕḥû*];
> they trusted [*bāṭĕḥû*], and you delivered them.
> To you they cried, and were saved;
> in you they trusted [*bāṭĕḥû*], and were not ashamed.

This three-fold sounding of the theme of trust, along with its vindication through God's deliverance, sets the stage for the psalmist's own case in vv. 9-10 (Heb. 10-11):

> You are the one who took me from the womb;
> you kept me safe [*mabṭîḥ*] upon my mother's breasts.

Upon you was I cast from my birth,
and since my mother bore me you have been my God.

The translation "kept me safe" renders the Hebrew verb *bāṭaḥ,* in its special form, "entrust" or "cause to trust." The imagery is telling. In the opening line of this passage the psalmist says, "you are the one who took me from the womb," while in the closing line he says, "my mother bore me." In and through the human agency of his birth he experienced the agency of God. Similarly, in the two enclosed lines the psalmist can speak at one and the same time of being entrusted upon "my mother's breasts" and of being cast "upon you." If the ancestors trusted in God and were delivered, so Job first learned trust when God, in another sense, delivered him.

It is the life-giving intimacy, and the organic bonds of implicit mutual trust and reciprocal generosity that grow up between a child and its parents, that inform the intensity and the anguish of the cry, "Why have you forsaken me? Why are you so far from helping me? . . . Be not far from me, for trouble is near. . . . You, O Lord, be not far off! O you my helper, hasten to my aid!" (In this context we may note the poignancy of Jesus' cry of dereliction on the cross in Mark 15:34 [quoting Psalm 22], following as it does his earlier prayer in the garden of Gethsemane [Mark 14:36], "Abba, Father, all things are possible to you; remove this cup from me; yet not what I will, but what you will.")

Job's Deepest Crisis

The crisis of abandonment is, if anything, more grave than the crisis of injustice. One evidence of this, I suggest, is Job's preoccupation with the issue of injustice. The dynamics of denial and displacement are by now familiar to us as strategies for coping with what cannot be borne directly in its own right. Denial and displacement differ from one another in the precise strategy involved, but they may be viewed as different forms of the basic strategy of distancing. (Recall my opening remarks on the function of the "long ago and far away" opening in Job 1:1.) In denial, one suppresses the pain entirely, banishing it from sight. In displacement, one allows the pain to emerge into consciousness but associates it with a problem that, however troublesome in its own right, can in some manner be acknowledged and engaged.

The difference between anguish over abandonment and anguish over injustice may be explored in terms of Robert Frost's distinction between griefs and grievances. One can argue over a grievance. One can take it to a grievance committee and have it adjudicated in hope of having it set right. To bolster one's case, one can search for supporting evidence and work on developing supporting arguments; and one can aggressively challenge the evidence and attack the arguments of one's opponents. All of this provides a clear focus for one's energies — energies fueled by feelings of anger and indignation over the injustice to which one has been subjected. But one cannot handle grief that way. A grief can only be lamented. The loss can only be undergone and borne, its pain poured out in expressions of loss and futile longings for the return of what has been lost. Of course one may object, on the basis of Elisabeth Kubler-Ross's work on death and dying, that the prospect of death and the utter loss it threatens can also evoke anger and bargaining. But that is my point: the anger and the bargaining are a deflection of the feelings of grief from one realm to another. Eventually the grief must simply be borne.

Frost developed his distinction between griefs and grievances in his essay "Introduction to E. A. Robinson's *King Jasper*." For example:

> A distinction must be made between griefs and grievances. Grievances are probably more useful than griefs. . . . Grievances are certainly a power and are going to be turned on. . . . But for me, I don't like grievances. I find I gently let them alone wherever published. What I like is griefs and I like them Robinsonianly profound. . . . He asserted the sacred right of poetry to lean its breast to a thorn and sing its dolefullest. . . . A few superficial irritable grievances, perhaps, as was only human, but these are forgotten in the depth of the griefs to which he plunged us. Grievances are a form of impatience. Griefs are a form of patience. . . .

Then, in a playful ironic jibe at those scientists who suppose that their discoveries and the application of those discoveries dispense with the need for religion, he continues:

> Desert religion for science, clean out the holes and corners of the residual unknown, and there will be no more need of religion. (Religion is merely consolation for what we don't know.) But suppose there was

some mistake, and the evil stood siege, the war didn't end, and something remained unknowable.[11]

To the degree that we can endure the loss of what we grieve for, to that degree we learn patience. Until we learn patience — until we learn to allow grief to work its slow healing ministry in us — we may displace the pain of our grief in the impatience of our grievances. The concern that arises over injustice is a placeholder for the concern that arises over loss. But it is not an empty placeholder; it also works for us in its own way. The concern for justice gives our wounded feelings a space and an opportunity for action, and the anger and indignation that fuels that action can help to rescue us from the depths of profound depression. So it is that Job's initial loss of appetite for life and wish to die shifts, through his argument with his friends and his desire for a day in court, to a gradual renewal of his energy. Speaking of himself in the face of his mockers and accusers, he can say (17:9),

> Yet the righteous holds to his way,
> and he that has clean hands grows stronger and stronger.

And whereas in ch. 3 he had cursed the day of his birth, visiting darkness henceforth upon it rather than the annual reappearance of its light, now he can say (as I translate and interpret it in my commentary),

> The desires of my heart make night into day:
> Light is near (they say) in the face of darkness. (17:11-12)[12]

But these evidences of growing strength are ambiguous in their significance. Insofar as they are fueled by his righteous indignation, they can be interpreted as expressing and indeed intensifying his bitterness. Job's preoccupation with the issue of injustice brings down on him the friends' preoccupation with his guilt. And their accusation compounds his suffering. His initial bitterness in 3:20 is the bitterness of raw grief. Under the impact of their preoccupation with issues of justice and injustice, his bitter grief festers and changes into moral bitterness. And, as we shall see in the next

---

11. *Collected Poems, Prose, & Plays,* 742-43.
12. J. Gerald Janzen, *Job.* Interpretation (Atlanta: John Knox, 1985).

chapter, moral bitterness is a potentially fatal spiritual state. Meanwhile, we may pause to consider the case of one of Job's biblical companions in bitterness.

Job's Soul Mate among Women

In the next chapter I will attempt to follow Job in his bitterness and trace how his oath enables him to move through it to a resolution of his plight in the divine speeches. For now, I want to draw attention to another biblical figure whose life began in fertility and prosperity and threatened to end in bitterness at the hands of Shadday. I am speaking, of course, of Naomi (*no'ŏmî*, "my sweet") in the book of Ruth.

We have already noted that the divine name Shadday occurs seven times in reference to the Genesis ancestors of Israel. Strikingly, of its 48 occurrences in the Old Testament as a whole, 31 fall in Job. The remaining 10 are sprinkled at rare intervals through the rest of the Old Testament. And the name comes, fittingly, to Naomi's lips as she laments her plight — famine in the land of her birth and the death of her husband and her two sons before they could father grandchildren for her.

> Do not call me Naomi ("my sweet"), call me Mara ("bitter"),
> for Shadday has dealt very bitterly with me.
> I went away full, and the Lord has brought me back empty.
> Why call me Naomi, when the Lord has afflicted me
> and Shadday has brought calamity upon me? (Ruth 1:20-21)

Her bitterness is the bitterness of her grief over the loss of her husband and sons: "I went away full, and the Lord has brought me back empty." In saying this she says what Job says in his initial exclamation that "the Lord gave and the Lord has taken away." But her attributions of this calamity to Yahweh are framed by her references to Shadday, and it is specifically as Shadday (as in Job 27:2) that God has embittered her.

But the ground for the healing of Naomi's bitterness has begun to be laid even before she voices this bitter cry. (We may note in passing the resonance between the townsfolk's question in Ruth 1:19, "Is this Naomi?" and the narrator's comment in Job 2:12 that when Job's friends first saw him "they did not recognize him.") In spite of her urging that her widowed daughters-in-law return to their own homeland and find husbands there, Ruth vows to stick with her in life and even in death. This expression of *hesed* — of a kin loyalty that has arisen through marriage — reverberates through the rest of the story until it finds its answering *hesed* in the kinsman Boaz. The celebration of the barley harvest — a manifestation of "the blessings of heaven above, blessings of the deep that couches beneath" (Gen 49:25) — is shortly followed by the marriage of Boaz and Ruth and, in short order, the manifestation of "blessings of the breasts and of the womb." How is Naomi's bitterness healed? The women, exclaiming over the birth of her grandson, say to her,

> He shall be to you a restorer of life and a nourisher of your old age;
> for your daughter-in-law who loves you,
> who is more to you than seven sons, has borne him. (Ruth 4:15)

Nothing is said here concerning any divine purpose in the earlier famine or the death of her husband and sons. Nothing is said here to address any grievance she may have lodged against divine justice. What is narrated is Naomi's restoration to life and nourishment in her old age. Though it is not stated, it is surely implied: Naomi will no longer call herself Mara. She is once again Naomi; her life has become sweetened once again. And how does it become sweetened?

> Then Naomi took the child and laid him in her bosom,
>   and became his nurse.
> And the women of the neighborhood gave him a name,
> saying, "A son has been born to Naomi." (4:16-17)

In offering to the infant boy the sweetness of her breast, her own *nepeš* is revived and sweetened at the hand of the God who enables her to nurse the child — a God that Gen 49:25 identifies as Shadday. And what will she convey to this child along with her milk and her crooning and her dandling and, eventually, as the weaned child comes to her for comforting? Will she not have learned to pray her own version of Psalm 131? And to convey to the little boy her own version of its concluding exhortation, "O Israel, hope in the Lord from this time forth and for evermore"? For she will know, as Moses and Israel learned after the crisis of the golden calf, that the covenantal face of Yahweh is informed by the parental heart of Shadday.

86

6. Job's Oath

In earlier chapters we have seen how Israel's story develops in two chief phases, ancestral and Mosaic. These two phases become narrative strands in which, however prominent a place the later one occupies much of the time, the earlier one continues as a sustaining undercurrent. (Interested readers may wish to read Robert Frost's poem "A Brook in the City.") And every now and then, in times of dire crisis, that undercurrent rises to the surface in such a way that its crucial vitality in Israel's relations with God becomes evident. Within this narrative context, we have seen how these two domains of experience and understanding run through the book of Job: most prominently, the legal domain of justice, law, and the courts; and less prominently, the domain of the family with its concerns.

The interplay of these two domains bears directly on Job's experience of bitterness, and gives that bitterness its significance for the whole story. As ch. 3 shows, his bitterness arises as raw, bewildered grief over his many losses and at that point is voiced in the context of a lament over the fact that he was ever conceived, birthed, and nursed at the breast. In his bitter misery Job longs for death and the grave, where the weary are at rest, the prisoners are at ease together, and slaves are free from their taskmasters (3:17-19). Such a state would be in striking contrast to his present condition, in which "I am not at ease, nor am I quiet; I have no rest" (3:26). But is it really death he wishes for — death simply as extinction and oblivion? In 1:21 he had said, "Naked I came from my mother's womb, and naked shall I return there." As commentators have noted, the "there" in 1:21 implies some sort of analogy between womb and tomb (an analogy hinted at also in Ps 139:13-18). And, as commentators have also noted, the "there" in 1:21 is echoed in the repeated "there" of 3:17-19. Insofar as Job here views the grave as a place of quiet rest and ease, his longing is in some sense not so much for death as for that primal place of dark quiet rest in which, before his birth, he first experienced his mother's care.

If Job's bitterness in 3:20 stands in contrast to the implicit sweetness of his mother's breast (3:12), in 6:2-7 he elaborates the "taste" of his current experience and of Eliphaz's first attempt to console him. But in 7:11 his bitterness becomes the ground of his first questions to God. And in 9:18 his accusation that God "will not let me get my breath, but fills [literally, 'sates'] me with bitterness" comes in the context of Job's first extended appeal for a trial. He longs for a trial, and yet he fears it, knowing that it will not be a fair trial. For God is both his accuser and his judge, and there is no impartial mediator (9:33). Why would his judge and accuser suddenly give him a fair hearing, if already now

> he crushes me with a tempest [śĕʿārâ, "whirlwind"],
> and multiplies my wounds without cause;
> he will not let me get my breath,
> but fills me with bitterness. (9:17)

Here we see the raw bitterness of his grief beginning to turn into moral bitterness over the injustice of his calamity (9:17-18). As we shall see, these two verses put in play themes and images that will recur at several strategic points later in the book. (In particular, the image of the whirlwind or tempest comes to its apotheosis in the speeches of God in chs. 38–41.)

In this chapter, now, I want to try to show how the two domains of experience, familial and political/legal, and the associated models of religious understanding come together in Job's oath in 27:1-6 in such a way that Job's moral bitterness opens itself up to healing and is assuaged.

Why Do We Need Oaths?

Where conclusive evidence for a crime is lacking, and a trial turns on the relative persuasiveness of human testimony on each side, accusers and their witnesses *swear* that their testimony is true, while defendants and their witnesses also swear that *their* testimony is true. What does the oath add that is not already there in the testimony itself? If I find myself capable of lying in the act of giving false testimony, what is to prevent me from lying in the act of taking an oath as to the "truth" of that false testimony? Likewise, if I do not believe the testimony of the witnesses on the other side, why should I take their oath as giving it credibility?

The need for oaths turns on the fact that we cannot see into other persons' hearts. Their moral and spiritual integrity is the only guarantee, humanly speaking, that what they say with their lips is the "outward and visible sign" of the "inward and spiritual truth" in their hearts. So when persons take an oath, they lay their moral and spiritual integrity on the line. We may note that the issue of integrity is one of the central themes in the book of Job. In Hebrew the word translated "integrity" is *tōm* or *tummâ*, "completeness, soundness." In English we do not have an adjective, "integrous," but in Hebrew the adjective is *tom* or *tāmîm,* "complete, sound." In sacrificial contexts the term refers to an animal without blemish. We are told, at the outset, that Job is "blameless" (*tom,* 1:1, 8). After his second calamity his wife says to him, "Do you still hold fast [*ḥāzaq*] to your integrity [*tumma*]? Curse God and die" (2:9). With this question we are alerted to the fact that Job's deepest ordeal consists in the challenge to his integrity, his wholeness as a person. When he comes to take the oath, in 27:1-6, he swears that "I will not put away my integrity [*tumma*] from me. I hold fast [*ḥāzaq*] my righteousness, and will not let it go." Job claims that what he has said throughout his argument with his friends, concerning his own innocence, is "the truth, the whole truth, and nothing but the truth."

But do we know the whole truth about ourselves? Is it not possible to be ignorant, or even self-deceiving, about our innermost memories and motivations? A wag has said that Freud's central insight into the human psyche can be summed up in the notion that the truth about ourselves is a secret we keep from ourselves. What hope, then, does anyone have, and what hope does any community have, of ever getting at the truth, in cases where grave charges and countercharges have been hurled and there is no evidence to back up either side? In a secular society, such cases may reach a point where, though decisions are handed down and sentences are carried out, a cloud of uncertainty continues to hang over the whole affair and nothing will ever remove it. In religious societies, the oath is made before God who knows the human heart through and through. Psalm 139 — probably an extended oath of innocence — is the most elaborate expression of this religious awareness and appeal. Interestingly, in that psalm the confession of openness to God, and the invitation for God to search the heart through and through, reaches its climax in the image of God as present already in one's conception and birth (Ps 139:13-18). The potential for paranoid terror at the prospect of God knowing me better than I know myself — a terror that could drive me to flee far from God, even into Sheol (139:7-12) — is mitigated by this recollection: the God who was present at my very conception, as the shaping and life-giving ground of my life, and whose knowledge of me is the knowledge of one who from that moment on cared for me (cf. Job 10:10-12), need not be dreaded, but may be trusted. For if God finds any wicked way in me God will not utterly condemn, but will "lead me in the way everlasting" (Ps 139:24).

(In passing, we may note how this dynamic informs the prayer with which Anglicans traditionally have opened all services of Holy Communion, where they come to God's table to be fed: "Almighty God, unto whom all hearts are open, all desires known, and from whom no secrets are hid, cleanse the thoughts of our hearts by the inspiration of thy Holy Spirit, that we may perfectly love thee and worthily praise thee." As in Psalm 139, the potential for paranoia in the sense of openness to God's knowing is assuaged by the trust that openness to God's knowing leads to cleansing and renewal.)

An oath, then, has both horizontal and vertical dimensions. Horizontally, an oath binds one to one's community in the claim that one is giving truthful witness concerning some issue in community relations. Vertically, an oath binds one to the God who alone can assess the truth of that claim. Since the oath arises in reference to those "secrets" of the heart that are known only to oneself and to God, and yet binds one to the community and to God, the oath is at one and the same time the most *solitary* and the most *solidary* act of which we are morally and spiritually capable. To lie under oath, therefore — to commit perjury — is to destroy our integrity, our wholeness. It is to tear ourselves apart into a half that speaks one thing and a half that knows another while claiming that both halves are one and the same. In that sense, the penalty for perjury is instantaneously visited on the perjurer, by the perjurer's own act, under God from whom the very dynamics of conscience proceed and are sustained.

Oaths in the Ancient Near East

In the ancient Near East, if people went around accusing you of being a wrong-doer, but refused to produce specifics of charge and evidence, you could appear before an official and swear what is called an oath of clearance, and then your detractors would be required to "put up or shut up." Either they must appear with you before an official with their evidence and/or witnesses, where the proceedings would determine innocence or guilt; or they must henceforth cease and desist from defaming you. Several scholars have recently brought this practice to bear on Job's case, most recently Carol Newsom in her commentary on Job in the *New Interpreter's Bible*. As Newsom and others point out, the whole legal and courtroom theme in the book of Job breaks down at the point of the oath.[1] Already in ch. 9 Job had identified the dilemma: How does one gain a fair hearing before a judge who is also one's accuser? This dilemma seems only to be exacerbated when Job takes an oath. Indeed, after what he has said in ch. 9, and often in following chapters, how can Job bring himself to subject himself to the searching scrutiny of a God who holds him guilty already despite his innocence?

In ch. 23, where Job once again bitterly voices his plea for a fair hearing (23:1-7), a momentary conviction that he will be vindicated (23:6-7, 10-12) gives way to feelings of overwhelming apprehension which move him to thoughts of flight like the speaker in Ps 139:7-12:

> But he stands alone and who can dissuade him?
> What he desires, that he does.
> For he will complete what he appoints for me;
> and many such things are in his mind.
> Therefore I am terrified at his presence;
> when I consider, I am in dread of him.
> God has made my heart faint;
> Shadday has terrified me.
> If only I could vanish in darkness,
> and thick darkness would cover my face!
>
> (23:13-17 NRSV, modified; see NAB)

What enables Job to approach such a God with such an oath as we hear in 27:1-6? Is it some kind of defiant Promethean self-assertion? I think not. Within the very words of his oath we may discern the same basis of trust that we see in Ps 139:13-18.

---

1. Carol A. Newsom, "The Book of Job," in *The New Interpreter's Bible*, 4 (Nashville: Abingdon, 1996) 522-23.

Job's Oath in 27:1-6

> And Job again took up his discourse, and said:
> "As God lives, who has taken away my right,
> and Shadday, who has made my soul bitter;
> as long as my breath [něšāma] is in me,
> and the spirit [rûaḥ] of God is in my nostrils,
> my lips will not speak falsehood,
> and my tongue will not utter deceit.
> Far be it from me to say that you are right;
> till I die I will not put away my integrity [tumma] from me.
> I hold fast my righteousness, and will not let it go;
> my heart does not reproach me for any of my days." (NRSV, modified)

As Carol Newsom points out in her commentary, oaths are normally taken in the name of God as giver or doer of some positive thing.[2] Here, Job swears in the name of God as one who has taken away his right and made his soul bitter. How can he swear an oath invoking such a God as witness and enforcer of the truth of his oath? How is it that his moral bitterness does not move him to close himself off completely from such a God and curl up in his own solitary sense of righteous indignation, where, like a rotting hazel nut inside its shell, his bitterness turns ever more rancid?

The ground of Job's willingness to swear such an oath — a ground so deeply hidden within him that it comes to expression only indirectly — appears in v. 3:

> as long as my breath is in me,
> and the spirit of God is in my nostrils.

The breath that Job uses to assert the oath is his own. It is at his disposal, to speak words of blessing and words of curse, words of agreement and words of disagreement, words of hope and words of despair. All such words he has already spoken at one point or another. His breath (the něšāma of Gen 2:7) is the very principle of life within him, and he now pours out the central conviction of his life in his oath of innocence. And yet, in that act he betrays an even deeper conviction — that even as he uses his breath to

2. Newsom, "The Book of Job," 522-23.

speak, that breath continues to be, as it was from birth, the breath or spirit that God gives him. So, deeper than the God who has embittered his soul is the God who continues to hold him in life, who continues, in fact, to empower him as he uses his breath to voice his complaints and his assertions of innocence. Here he touches the experiential truth he had voiced in 10:9-12. Here — though it does not enter into his consciousness — the spirit of God is in his nostrils like the water at the scent of which the tree that has been cut down revives and will flourish again (14:7-9).

I recall a situation once in which, as I thought, some parental insistence was called for. Violin practice had not been pursued as diligently as might have been hoped, and so the lesson scheduled for later that day was being resisted. Every effort on my daughter's part to indicate why the lesson would be a waste of time was met by a calm but firm parental reason as to why it should nevertheless occur. Finally, when attempts on both sides to be reasonable had exhausted themselves, I said with parental peremptoriness, "Get your coat and come along; we're going." At which point, my eleven-year-old daughter sank back in the couch like a cornered mouse, her eyes blazed, and she said with urgent intensity, "I hate you, Daddy!" Whoa! Wrong course of action! Not on her part; on mine. There was no lesson for her that day; that issue was resolved in other ways. The lesson that day was for me. That my daughter would confront me in that way left me shaken to the core and at the same time profoundly thankful. The "I hate you!" that belonged to that specific occasion and its issues was grounded in and made possible by a relationship named in the word "Daddy," a word that voiced what she was appealing to in me and also the ground in herself that gave her the trust and courage to make that appeal as well as that accusation.

Something like that is what I see in Job's oath. His primal trust in the God who gave and gives him breath enables him both to assert his innocence and his integrity before God and, at the same time, to submit that claim to God for adjudication. One sign that this oath does not issue in the loss of his integrity, but in its validation, is the outcome in chs. 29–30. In ch. 3 his calamities had moved him to rue his life and to curse the day of his birth and the night of his conception. Such a curse had torn a rent between his past and his present. In view of his present misery and bitterness of soul, what had earlier seemed to be a wonderful gift of life now was turned to dust and ashes. But in ch. 29 he is able to view the past in quite another light. Despite all that he is now suffering, he finds that he can long for a life such as he once knew and still affirm:

93

> Oh, that I were as in the months of old,
> as in the days when God watched over me;
> when his lamp shone upon my head,
> and by his light I walked through darkness;
> as I was in my autumn days,
> when the friendship of God was upon my tent;
> when Shadday was yet with me,
> when my children were about me;
> when my steps were washed with milk,
> and the rock poured out for me streams of oil! (29:2-6)

Job's appetite for life, turned so bitter since 3:20 and 6:4-7, has returned, and not by way of an escape from the present into the past. For, as ch. 30 shows, he can make that affirmation in full view of his present misery. Among the various things that his integrity consists in, it consists in his ability, finally now, both to embrace the goodness of his former life and to acknowledge the badness of his present life — extremes that he is not able to comprehend with his mind but that he can at least admit into his heart, side by dissonant side. (Musicians will affirm that in the context of a musical composition dissonance can be a form — albeit a strange form — of compatibility in Alfred North Whitehead's sense, as a discordant clash of notes that can be felt or heard and accepted at one and the same time.)

That integrity, flowing from the act of challenge and trusting self-submission in 27:1-6, enacts itself again in ch. 31, in the even more elaborate oath before the God whom he again names as Shadday. With this extended oath, he finally stops speaking: "The words of Job are ended [*tammû*]." Are they simply brought to a conclusion? Or does that final verb, *tammû*, carry an additional connotation, one not only of completion but also of wholeness, of integrity? If we may hear these words, not as those of some narrator, but as Job's own, they may constitute Job's final claim of integrity and his final submission of that claim to God's adjudication. For that adjudication we must turn to the divine speeches in chs. 38–41.

7. God's Response, Job's Response, and Final Resolution

In this book I have been exploring aspects of biblical religion as they reflect and bear upon two domains of human experience, the familial and the political. In the previous chapter I tried to show how these two domains are engaged in Job's oath of 27:1-6 and then more elaborately in ch. 31. In swearing such an oath, Job places himself within the domain of politics and the law, of which courts and oaths are part of the institutional machinery. In this domain, where accuser and accused appear before a judge, one party's case is upheld and the other party's case is not. In this domain, both parties cannot be right, or "in the right." For every winner there is a loser, and justice in this setting is a "zero sum" game where the debits and the credits balance each other out.

As I noted earlier, the law-court imagery that Job introduced in chs. 9–10, and returned to repeatedly, breaks down if God is both judge and accuser, for in that case there is no hope of an impartial and fair trial. In 9:32-33 Job had said, "He is not a man, as I am, that I might answer him, that we should come to trial [*mišpāṭ*] together. There is no umpire [*mōkîaḥ*] between us, who might lay his hand upon us both." How is it, then, that Job, knowing this, has the courage to take such an oath? In 9:34-35 he had said, "Let him take his rod away from me, and let not dread of him terrify me. Then I would speak without fear of him, for I am not so in myself." What is it that has overcome this fear to enable him, in taking the oath, to expose and bind himself to the judgment of his accuser?

The key to Job's courage lies in how he invokes God in taking the oath. He might have invoked God (as Abraham does in Gen 18:25) as "the judge of all the earth." But that oath would leave Job completely within the domain of law and its logic. Instead, Job swears by Shadday, who has embittered Job yet whose spirit is in Job's nostrils as his own breath. That is, he swears in the name of the God whose domain is heaven and earth and whose characteristic activity is the blessing of heaven and earth to render them fruitful and capable of sustaining all life in them, as also the blessing of breast and womb so as to bring forth life within them. In swearing by Shadday, Job stands *within* the domain of the court and its laws but he stands *upon* the primal relation with God that goes deeper than those laws, a relation for which the ethos of family relations provides the more adequate imagery. Rooted in this domain, he is enabled to reach down past his own bitterness to a depth within himself where God's life-giving presence (like the scent of water in 14:9) enables him to entrust himself in and through his oath to the verdict that God will render. And how does God respond?

God in the Courtroom and in the Whirlwind

In our preoccupation with *what* God says to Job in chs. 38–41, it is easy to overlook *how* God says it to him. God begins by speaking to Job "out of" a whirlwind. One frequent line of interpretation is to take the whirlwind as indicating God's blustering attempt to intimidate Job, overwhelm his arguments with sheer force, and, as we might put it in a current colloquialism, "blow him away." This would merely confirm Job's worst suspicions voiced in ch. 9. Along with such an interpretation one often hears the complaint that God does not answer Job's questions about justice. As I have come to read the divine speeches, such interpretations and such complaints miss the point. Just as Job's oath arises within the domain of the law and its courts but then moves outside that domain into the deeper domain of Shadday, so the divine speeches arise within the same courtroom domain but then take Job out of that domain into the domain of Shadday, in the process giving the term "justice" *(mišpāṭ)* a different connotation.

The first divine speech ends in 40:1 with God's question, "Shall a faultfinder contend with Shadday? He who argues with God, let him answer it." The Hebrew verb translated "faultfinder" frequently refers to the action of bringing a case against someone. And the English words "he who argues" translate the Hebrew participle *môkîah*, which in 9:33 was translated "umpire." If Job has been viewing God as both accuser and judge, here God takes up a position as defendant before Job, whose previous words God takes as the words of an accuser and judge of God! How does God the defendant respond to Job's charges?

The first requirement in a witness is presence at the scene of the crime, so that the witness can testify to what has been seen firsthand. But, says God to Job, "Where were you when I laid the foundations of the earth?" (38:4). How can Job testify to the purpose and manner of God's creative action, if Job was not there from the outset? The first requirement in a judge and accuser of wrongdoing is a knowledge of what would constitute right action. But in regard to the creation and continuous operation of a cosmos, who can claim, on the basis of one's own cosmic creativity, to know what such right action should look like? Has Job ever commanded a morning, or cleft a channel for the rain, let alone set bounds for the sea? To adapt a saying introduced earlier, God's response to Job's accusations may be summed up in the words, "Them as can, does; them as can't, criticize." In these ways, God calls into question Job's credentials for calling into question the rightness of God's way of designing and running the cosmos.

Then, in 40:8, at the beginning of the second speech, God asks Job, "Will you even put me in the wrong? Will you condemn me that you may be justified?" The old translation, in the King James Version, catches the first question more precisely: "Wilt thou also disannul my judgment [*mishpat*]?" The second may be translated, "Will you put me in the wrong that you may be declared in the right?" It is possible to take these questions as posed solely within the domain of courtroom procedure and its logic, the logic of the zero-sum game where for one party to be declared in the right the other party must be declared in the wrong. But I think something else is going on here. Given how the divine speeches have to do primarily with the dynamic processes at work in God's creation, and in this way move out of the domain of law and its courts and into the domain of Shadday, I think God is asking Job to relinquish his zero-sum understanding of *mišpāt*. So I propose the following paraphrase of the second question, turning it into a statement: "Job, you don't have to put me in the wrong in order for you to be vindicated against the charges of your friends. But in order for you to appreciate this, you have to relinquish your understanding of ultimate divine justice and see it rather in terms of the dynamic thrust toward life that you see manifest in the world around you. This understanding of my *mišpāt* does not rule out the possibility of undeserved suffering; but it places it within a context which will free you from the logic of your friends." To see how this is implied, it will be helpful to compare the openings of the two speeches, in 38:2-3 and 40:7-8, and then to compare these openings with the opening of the divine speech to exilic Israel in Isa 40:12-31. But before I do that, there is one bit of unfinished business to attend to, in regard to the significance of names and titles for God.

Interlude: On "Shadday" and "Yahweh" in Job 38:1–42:6

On the basis of God's self-identification in Job 40:2 I have been taking the divine speeches to be uttered by God as Shadday. But in 38:1; 40:1, 3, 6; and 42:1 the narrator identifies God as "the Lord," that is, "Yahweh." How might this affect our reading of this exchange between Job and God?

Let us, for the moment, associate "Yahweh" with the domain of law and order as covenanted on Mount Sinai. In this case, the narrator names God appropriately, insofar as God, taking up Job's courtroom language, takes up a position as defendant in that court before Job's accusations. But when God speaks to Job, God's self-identification in 40:2 is one of the signals that God's response to Job does not stay there, but moves (and seeks to move Job) into the domain fundamentally associated with Shadday — the domain of cosmic and human blessing.

The Issue in Job 38:2-3 and 40:7-8

In respect to their form, these two passages contain the same ingredients: (1) a challenge to Job, reiterated in identical words (38:3; 40:7); and (2) equivalent questions defending against the effect of Job's charges against God. The equivalent questions are these:

> Who is this that darkens counsel ['ēṣâ]?
> Will you also disannul my judgment [mišpāt]?

By appearing in equivalent questions in the respective speech-openings, the two words 'ēṣâ and mišpāt function as close synonyms, or as closely related alternates, for describing God's way of designing and running the world.

Now, intriguingly, there is only one other place in the Bible where the terms *'ēṣâ* and *mišpāṭ* occur together like this. That place is Isa 40:12-14, where God mounts a response to Jacob/Israel, who, in the midst of the sufferings of the exile, complains, "My way is hid from the Lord, and my right [*mišpāṭ*] is disregarded by my God" (Isa 40:27). Concerns over the question of *mišpāṭ* run through this exilic prophet (Isaiah 40–55), as the frequent occurrence of this word shows (40:14, 27; 41:1; 42:1, 3, 4; 49:4; 50:8; 51:4; 53:8; 54:17). Tellingly, the word occurs most frequently in relation to the figure of God's servant, in Isaiah 42, 49, 50, and 53, portrayals that involve an increasingly explicit reference to that righteous figure's undeserved sufferings in God's service. What is so intriguing is that those portrayals, suggesting a divine *mišpāṭ* that boggles the mind of conventional ruling wisdom (Isa 52:15–53:1), are rooted and grounded in God's acts of cosmic creation (Isa 40:12-14). So it is not surprising that the words in Isa 55:8, "My thoughts are not your thoughts, neither are your ways my ways," are preceded by a proclamation of God's mercy and pardon on all wicked and unrighteous persons who draw near, and they are followed by a celebration of the efficacy of the divine word in the imagery of rain and snow that come down from heaven to water the earth and enable it to become fruitful so as to sustain all life on it. The *mišpāṭ* the God of Second Isaiah visits upon the wicked and unrighteous is, upon their repentance and return, the blessing of the renewal of their participation in the life of the cosmos. The theme of cosmic renewal that runs through Second Isaiah in images of "streams in the desert" and lush new vegetation stands out against the introductory image, in Isa 40:6-8, of what happens to grass when "the breath of the Lord" blows upon it. It is generally recognized that this image draws on the effect of the hot east wind, or sirocco, upon spring flowers in that region of the world. This image brings us back to the divine speeches in Job.

The God of the Whirlwind

We are prone to read the divine speeches as direct divine verbal communications, in which God speaks to Job *about* various aspects of creation. But let us attend more closely to what the text says: "Then the Lord answered Job *out of the whirlwind*" (38:1). It is in the whirlwind, and through it, that Job hears God speaking to him. The most natural way to imagine this is in analogy with the scenario we encounter in Psalm 29. In this psalm "the voice of the Lord" is heard in the sound of the thunder, the forceful movement of the wind, and the lightning flashes of a storm that sweeps across the Mediterranean waters (Ps 29:3), eastward onto the coastland where it encounters the cedars of Lebanon (29:5-6), and further on eastward into the desert interior (29:8). A so-called neutral observer, or person from Mars, not having been raised in the religious traditions of the time, would perceive only the thunder, wind, and lightning. But those in the temple who cry "Glory!" (Ps 29:9) perceive something else. They hear God speaking to them and burst forth in rejoicing. For in these natural processes they hear and see evidence of God acting to render the earth fertile and life-sustaining. The content of that message, I suggest, is identical to the message Job hears in the divine speeches. And the message comes to Job, as it does in Psalm 29, in and through not only the whirlwind but also in and through the natural processes that the divine speeches go on to portray.

What, then, is it about the whirlwind that occasions such an inbreaking into Job's consciousness with all the force, illumination, and resolution of divine address?

What is it in this whirlwind that leads him to hear all that follows in chs. 38–41? Here we must pause, again, and reflect on how different persons experience weather in different ways.

I grew up in Saskatchewan, which for many decades carried on its license plates the motto "The Wheat Province." Saskatchewan's economy for a long time was primarily agricultural, its prosperity utterly dependent on rain at the right time. One year the spring seeding was followed by early showers ("the blessings of heaven above," in the words of Gen 49:25). But then a long dry spell set in, and crop experts announced that if rain did not come within a few days the entire grain crop would fail with devastating economic consequences. That Sunday afternoon a family took me home to dinner after the morning worship (I was their student pastor). We had no sooner stepped inside their front door when it began to rain; and the rain continued to fall softly, off and on, for three days. Relief! Joy! But I could imagine the folk in the city who, having worked all week in their offices, grumbled at the tennis matches they had to forgo that weekend. What was a blessing to the farmers was frustration to these office workers. What would the whirlwind connote to a person living in Job's day? What in the message of the whirlwind would sound such a note of joy that the very stars seemed to sing (Job 38:7)?

In his last words before he elaborated his oath, in 30:29-31, Job had lamented becoming "a brother of jackals, and a companion of ostriches," a self-description that placed him existentially in the wilderness. His further lament, "My skin turns black and falls from me, and my bones burn with heat," placed him in a Middle Eastern summer. The lament itself he characterized this way: "My lyre is turned to mourning, and my pipe to the voice of those who weep." When he experiences the onset of this whirlwind, the effect is not to intensify his mourning, but to cause him to hear a different tune, the sound of joy and singing. It is not too much to say that Job is not far from the psalmist's confession, "You have turned for me my mourning into dancing, you have loosed my sackcloth and girded me with gladness" (Ps 30:11). (With the note of joy and singing in Job 38:7 we may compare the repeated references to the singing of nature in Isa 42:10, 11; 44:23; 49:13; 52:9; 55:12.) But what in the whirlwind would enable the beginnings of such a turn?

When we see the word "whirlwind," we may be inclined to think of a "twister," a tornado or other highly destructive circular wind. The Hebrew term *sĕʿārâ* in Job 38:1 and 40:6 means, simply, a strong wind. More specifically, it refers to the hot east wind that sweeps westward across the south Arabian peninsula and comes upon the eastern Mediterranean coast with variable significance depending on the season of the year. A bit of meteorology will help to clarify the picture we should imagine Job caught up in.

Job and the Lord of the East Wind

The region along the eastern Mediterranean coast is marked by two major seasons, summer (hot and dry) and winter (rainy), with two shorter "interchange" periods that mark the transition from one to the other. The weather systems involving wind are of two sorts, one coming from the northwest and bringing rain, the other (a "sirocco") a hot, dry wind coming from the southeast. The two shorter "interchange" periods are so called because they are marked by alternations between the eastern, hot and dry winds and the western, rain-bringing winds. Plowing and seeding take place during the last stages of the winter season. The end of this season is marked by the onset of the east wind whose heat kills floral vegetation (see the imagery in Isa 40:6-8) and, with its accompanying dust, air pressure, and other features, makes life unpleasant and sometimes causes illness and even death. For about fifty days the two weather systems alternate, and then they subside into the long hot, dry summer. In the spring interchange, then, the east wind carries negative connotations.

But in the fall the east wind carries quite a different message. Its first onset signals the end of the hot, dry summer and the coming of the first rains from the west. In one observation, a first fall east wind was followed within two hours by a heavy ten-minute rain accompanied by thunder and lightning, and this in turn was followed two or three hours later by the return of the east wind. One author quotes Palestinian sayings that observe, "the east wind arouses the west wind," "the east wind brings the west wind," and "at the beginning of the year [where New Year's Day comes in the fall] the east wind is good."[1]

With this meteorological information let us now reflect back over the book of Job. His calamities begin with a report that Sabean raiders fell upon Job's servants while they were plowing. This implies a seasonal setting in the late winter or early spring. The second calamity takes the form of "fire of God" — that is, lightning — coming down from the sky. Chaldeans are responsible for a third calamity — being, like the Sabeans, an eastern people. The fourth and final calamity takes the form of "a great wind . . . across the wilderness" — that is, a powerful east wind. The fifth calamity to strike Job is an outbreak of terrible sores over his whole body. If the natural calamities occurred during the onset of the spring interchange season, we may understand Job's physical affliction as a not uncommon result of a particularly severe sirocco — the very wind that killed his children.

With this imagery in mind, our eyes are alerted for meteorological imagery in the chapters that follow, and we are not disappointed. Without attempting to trace this theme in all its occurrences, we may note its appearance in 9:17-18, where Job complains, "He crushes me with a tempest [$š^c\bar{a}r\hat{a}$], and multiplies my wounds without cause; he will not let me get my breath, but fills me with bitterness." Throughout the dialogues, Job and his friends frequently employ images of water and fertility on the one hand and dessication and wilderness on the other. And Elihu, who goes on and on almost endlessly in his youthful attempt to inform his elders of his own

---

1. Aloysius Fitzgerald, F.S.C., *The Lord of the East Wind.* Catholic Biblical Quarterly Monograph Series 34 (Washington: Catholic Biblical Association of America, 2002) 12, quoting Gustaf Dalman, *Arbeit und Sitte in Palästina* 1 (Gütersloh: Evangelischer, 1928) 103-4, 107.

"inspired" insights (32:8, 18; 33:4), finally, in celebrating God's wisdom and power, speaks of God's activity in the weather that brings rain, thunder, and lightning (36:24-33). Elihu becomes so caught up in his own description that it is as though he actually experiences the onset of such weather, in which (as in Psalm 29) he hears the thunder of God's voice (37:2-5) followed by rain (37:6). In the midst of this description of the awesomeness of such weather, he pauses to say, "Whether for correction, or for his land, or for love, he causes it to happen" (37:13).

Let us suppose that we are to hear the dialogues between Job and his friends as stretching over the long, hot summer. His intermittent hopes arise as a longing for "the scent of water" (14:7-9); but his final self-description leaves him still in scorching misery (30:29-31). Is it possible that Elihu's language about God and the weather, in 36:24–37:24, arises as he becomes subliminally aware of an imminent change in the weather? And is it possible that the divine speeches mark the onset of that weather? If so, what message does it bring?

In the first instance, what the "whirlwind," or sirocco, with its following rains, says to Job is that God is concerned, as Elihu has said, with "his land." The land exists not only for human purposes, but to sustain all life; and so God sends rain in the uninhabited wilderness (38:25-27) to provide fodder for wildlife to flourish in and for itself and entirely apart from human utility (39:5-12). But this weather that renews the earth also comes as a message to Job and humankind generally, and the message has a twofold character. It comes for "correction," and it comes for "love." Let us pause on these last two words.

The word "correction" in KJV, RSV, and NRSV translates Hebrew *shevet,* which refers literally to a "rod." Such a rod can be used to beat out grain, and it can be used to administer punishment. It can signify a ruler's authority, and it also serves as the rod or cane of an instructor. In Isa 11:4 the anointed king will "strike the earth with the rod of his mouth." What does this mean in this context? Is the rod here punitive? Or is it instructive? The wicked, it appears, are dealt with through the words of this royal figure who "decides with equity for the meek of the earth" in exercising the "wisdom and understanding, counsel and might, knowledge and fear of the Lord" bestowed on him by the Spirit of God (Isa 11:1-3). In this passage, then, the "rod" is not so much a physical instrument for beating others into submission, but words of wisdom that in their utterance judge on behalf of the poor and meek and undo the power of the wicked. I suggest that the "rod" in Job 37:13 carries that "wisdom" connotation. Who is being instructed? In a later chapter I will suggest that this voice from the whirlwind addresses also Job's friends, in 42:7. But first, the whirlwind and its following rain address Job. And clearly, insofar as the rain is life-renewing, it is not a punishing "correction." Rather, it corrects Job in respect to his assumption that God's justice is a zero-sum game locked within the logic of reward and punishment. But finally, the whirlwind and all that follows it carry to Job a message concerning God's "love," God's *hesed* or faithful, steadfast loyalty to both creation and Job himself. He who had briefly hoped for the scent of water now experiences it, in and through the renewal of the natural world around him in the coming of the fall rains.

The Comfort of the Friends and the Comfort of God

Before pursuing the significance of this experience for Job, I want to back up and review the contrast between God in the divine speeches and the friends who first make their appearance in ch. 2. In that chapter, they come "to condole with him and comfort him." These two verbs call for close attention. The first, Hebrew *nûd*, refers basically to bodily movement, as when a reed is moved by the action of wind and water (1 Kgs 14:15) or as when one shakes one's head in sympathy with another's plight. Such a movement of the body enacts what the word "sympathy" originally means, to identify at a deep bodily level of feeling with the plight of another. The second, Hebrew *niham*, refers basically to a change of heart and mind in respect to some action or event, either in retrospect or prospect. Where the action is a wrong one has committed, the verb in one form signifies the change of heart and mind we call repentance. Where the verb is used in another form to indicate one party's attempt to bring about a change of heart and mind in respect to something that has happened, it may (as here) be translated "to comfort." The passive use of the latter form then means "to be comforted," that is, to undergo a change of heart and mind concerning what has happened.

Job's state of heart and mind at the end of ch. 2 is something many can identify with. To be gripped by his calamities in all their specificity of detail can move the reader, like the friends, to simply shake one's head in a primal sympathy for which there are no words and to become aware of a perplexing mystery for which one has no explanation. To be caught up in this scene, as the friends are, can move the reader to want simply to "hold these matters in one's heart" and wait on whatever agencies of comfort may manifest themselves in time.

So the friends not only shake their heads, but they also enact the rituals of loss and grief appropriate in their cultural setting, tearing their clothes and sprinkling dust on their heads. Then they sit with Job in silence for seven days. When he finally breaks his silence in their presence, he names with great poignancy the state of soul which their desire to identify with and comfort is to address: he is in a state of misery and bitterness of soul (3:20). The second phrase, as we have seen, roots in one's sense of taste. Life, which had been sweet, now has taken on a bitter taste. The first phrase, "him that is in misery," translates the Hebrew adjective *ʿāmēl*. This word is derived from a verb which means "to exert oneself, to labor." Functioning as a noun, the adjective refers to "a laborer," one who "toils" (Eccl 2:22); and here in Job 3 it describes Job as, in the words of one dictionary, "burdened with grief." In recent years we have accustomed ourselves to the phrase "doing one's grief work." The stress of great calamity is not only emotionally wrenching; it is physically exhausting and wears one down in body and spirit. In such a case the task of family and friends is to help one simply keep going when what has happened threatens to empty life of any reason, or energy (see 6:11-13), for going on. The challenge to the friends is that, at present, Job's "consolation" (6:10) would be simply to die.

As we have already seen, Eliphaz and Bildad initially try to offer him sympathetic support and to encourage him with forms of hope. But their words, even after seven days, are premature; and their attempts to give too clear a theological interpretation of his experience only serve to provoke his theological questioning. From there on, the conversation turns into a theological debate centering in explanation, and rather than helping Job this debate only adds to the agonizing labor and travail of his soul (16:2, where "miserable" again translates *ʿāmāl*).

We may contrast these efforts of the friends with the response, in 42:11, of Job's brothers and sisters and old acquaintances. They too come to "condole with him and comfort him" (the expressions in 2:11 and 42:11 are identical). But nothing is said by way of attempted theological explanation. They eat with him in his house, and each of them gives him a piece of money and a ring of gold. In my youth, when a farmer's barn or house burned down, neighbors pitched in to help rebuild. This response, on the part of "theologically illiterate" people, is virtually universal. I suggest that this response implicitly embodies God's "theological" response in the divine speeches. No explanation, for what explanation could help to assuage the bitterness? Any explanation would only "justify" what had happened, by trying to make sense out of it within a scheme of things that can be fully understood. All God does is present a world that kindles in Job an appetite for going on with life, and that in so doing assuages his bitterness. It is a world filled with the renewal of vitality that rain brings — rain being to the earth what the money and pieces of gold bring to Job, and the feasting of the animals on the vegetation and animal life sustained by the rain being in nature what the meal of his friends with him affords to Job.

This does not erase Job's grief. Such grief as he has undergone never leaves the heart. Jacob gives voice to a universal experience when he says, of the supposed death of Joseph, "I shall go down to Sheol to my son, mourning" (Gen 37:35). But it is possible for the bitterness of the grief to undergo, in time, a sea change from bitterness to something else — a precious, tender treasuring still of what was lost, testifying to the way in which love can prove as strong as death (Song 8:6) and working a widening of one's capacity for compassion and primal sympathy with others.

One sign of this is Job's dealing with his friends, whose increasingly accusatory tirades, trapping him within a logic of reward and punishment, had only added to his misery and bitterness. But before I come to Job's final actions toward the friends, I want to back up and consider God's.

In 42:7, God says to the friends, "My wrath is kindled against you and against your two friends; for you have not spoken of [*'el*] me what is right, as my servant Job has." This verse has troubled many interpreters, who find it hard to square what God says here *about* Job with what God has just said *to* Job. There, God had accused Job of speaking nonsense about God, yet here God affirms what Job has said. My interpretation turns on a reconsideration of how to translate the Hebrew preposition *'el,* which in this verse is generally rendered "about." This preposition, which occurs more than 5,500 times in the Hebrew Bible, basically refers to motion towards something or someone. When it follows the verb *dibber,* "to speak," it almost always indicates the party *to whom* the subject of the verb is speaking. In a very few instances it appears to refer to something said *about* that party. But of the 150 occurrences of this verb followed by this preposition and a personal pronoun, in 149 instances the preposition means "to." I (along with one or two other interpreters)[2] take it in the same sense here: "You have not spoken to me in the right way as my servant Job has." What might that mean?

I take the reference here to be specific to the courtroom scenario that Job introduced in ch. 9 and that he returned to repeatedly until, in its climactic appearance, he, as it were, actually placed himself in that setting with his oath of clearance. When God speaks of Job as speaking in the right way *to* God, I take God to refer here to Job's willingness, in swearing his innocence, to subject himself, through the oath, to God's judgment and verdict. In this context, what was the appropriate role of Job's friends? At the very end of his final words, Eliphaz inadvertently indicated what he and his two associates ought to have been doing all along. For there he describes a Job who is right with God as praying to God and being heard (22:27), for (as NRSV correctly translates 22:30) "He will deliver even those who are guilty; they will escape because of the cleanness of your hands." The friends ought to have appeared in the divine court as character witnesses and as advocates on his behalf, supporting his claims before God. Or, if they considered him guilty, they should have interceded on his behalf, like Moses on behalf of Israel in Exodus 32. Instead, they have witnessed against him (Job 10:17; 19:2-22), so that his only hope, forlorn as it sounds, is that heaven will witness on his behalf (16:19; 19:23-27). And in the divine speeches heaven does. For, though they deny Job's charges against God, nothing in these speeches accuses Job of the sort of wrongdoing the friends have insinuated.

It is this the friends' false witness against Job that kindles God's wrath. (Cf. the structures against false witness in Exod 20:16; 23:1-2; Lev 5:1; and esp. Deut 19:15-19.) Insofar as they have failed Job in this fundamental act of human solidarity, by the terms of their own theology (and in accordance with Deut 19:15-19) God should deal with them in the very way they had said God deals with the wicked. But God doesn't. Instead, God sets Job forth as the very intercessory figure on their behalf that they ought to have been for him. They are to take sacrificial offerings, as expressions of their

---

2. Manfred Oeming, "Ihr habe nicht recht von mir geredet wie mein Knecht Hiob," *Evangelische Theologie* 60 (2000): 103-16, esp. 114. Siegfried Wagner, "Theologischer Versuch über Ijob 42,7-9(10a)," in *Alttestamentlicher Glaube und Biblische Theologie: Festschrift für Horst Dietrich Preuss zum 65. Geburtstag*, ed. Jutta Hausmann and Hans-Jürgen Zobel (Stuttgart: Kohlhammer, 1992) 216-24, esp. 220-21.

repentance, and have Job offer them on their behalf. And if Job prays for them, God will accept his prayer.

Why does God take this circuitous route and not simply forgive the friends outright, in a unilateral divine action? It is for the same reason, I suggest, that God did not answer the Satan's accusations against Job unilaterally, but involved Job in the refutation of those actions. In a conventional conception of divine ruling power and wisdom, as reiterated by Eliphaz, God ultimately trusts no one (4:18; 15:15). While God may work through heavenly and earthly underlings, even there God must govern the universe through fear (as Bildad restates Eliphaz's argument in 25:2-6). But God's trust in his "servant Job" is such that he waits on Job to prove the Satan wrong; and in his concluding oaths, in which he entrusts the adjudication of his case to God despite the bitterness he takes God to have administered to him, Job does just that. Now, God trusts Job to respond to his friends, not with a "personal injury claim" involving damages for all the pain they have added to his affliction, but with a compassionate plea on their behalf.

What enables Job to do this? Bitterness would dictate the personal injury claim. The fact that he prays for the friends shows that what he has experienced in and through the whirlwind and the rain that follows has worked in him a change of heart and mind. That change was already voiced in 42:6, a verse whose translation turns on how one interprets the larger scenario unfolding before the reader.

The KJV translates 42:6, "Therefore I despise *myself,* and repent in dust and ashes." As the italics indicate, the word "myself" has no Hebrew equivalent and is inserted to fill out the meaning the translators take the clause to have. Marvin Pope, in his Anchor Bible commentary, translates the first verb with "recant," meaning that Job despises and rejects, or recants, the accusations he had made against God.[3] The second verb, usually translated "repent," is a form of the verb that we first encountered in 2:11 and encounter for the last time in 42:11. In those passages it functions actively in the meaning "to comfort." Here, appearing in the passive-reflexive form, it can mean either "to repent" or "to take comfort, to be comforted." I take it in the latter sense. What Job experiences in the renewal of nature through the onset of the fall rains is a sense of comfort. So awesome is the vision of creation that he is taken out of himself and caught up in the won-

3. Marvin H. Pope, *Job.* Anchor Bible 15 (Garden City: Doubleday, 1965) 288.

der of a world teeming, once again, with life. The panorama that spreads before him is not a scene of human activity and human concerns as expressed in all the characteristic ways humans have of organizing their world to their own ends. The rain falls on the desert where no humans live, simply to render the desert verdant. Lions — so often emblems and embodiments of what threatens human life — here have their appetites satisfied by God. Asses and oxen — those beasts so often domesticated and put to human service — here range freely on the plain and in the mountains as in pastures God has provided for them. Confounding human common sense, ostriches lay their eggs on the ground where beasts might crush them. It is as though God is inviting Job to take his place in a world whose dynamism, in all its potential for vibrant life and, yes, danger, bursts through human concerns for "security first," concerns that help to fuel the human preoccupation with order and laws and reward-punishment logics. It is as though God is inviting Job to give up the logic of reward-punishment for a life-affirming strategy of risk-reward, in which affirmation of life in the face of all its vulnerabilities is the path to true participation in the mystery of existence.

This leads to a further word on the translation of 42:6. I suspect that the translation "*in* dust and ashes," as though these elements are symbols of his repentance, is dictated by the interpretation of the preceding verb as "I repent." But, of the dozens of times this Hebrew verb is followed by this Hebrew preposition, *ʿal,* "on, upon, over, on account of, concerning," never otherwise does the preposition refer to a location for the action of the verb — as though, in this instance, Job were to be imagined repenting while sitting on a heap of dust and ashes. (In 2:8, Job sits not on but "among" — *bĕtôk* — the ashes.) In the great majority of the instances in which this verb and this preposition occur, they have to do with the subject of the verb undergoing a change of mind *concerning* some state of affairs. Now, the phrase "dust and ashes" has occurred once before in this book. Significantly, it occurs in ch. 30, where Job contrasts his present miserable state with his former life. Bereft of human sympathy (30:1-15, 24-31), he turns to God (30:16-23), in his affliction pouring out his soul in complaint (cf. Ps 42:4; 62:8; 142:2). In his complaint he repeats the charge he had made in ch. 9. There, lamenting that God "crushes me with a tempest" (9:17), he had complained that despite attempts to show God clean hands, God would just plunge him into a pit that would so soil him that even his own clothes would abhor him (9:30-31). In 30:19-20 Job takes up this theme and laments, "God has cast me into the mire, and I have become like dust and ashes. I cry to thee and thou dost not answer me." But in the present "tempest," or whirlwind, God does answer him, in the rain for which his roots had longed. And God's answer does not plunge him into the mire. God has not rendered him mere dust and ashes. This, I take it, is what Job means in 42:6: He recants what he has charged God with, and he is comforted concerning his miserable state as set forth so poignantly in ch. 30. What lies before him, as he witnesses the renewal of the earth, is the possibility that he might have the wish expressed so wistfully in ch. 29 — simply, a return to the ordinary goodness of life. Though he is none the wiser as to how to explain his experiences, he is renewed in his appetite for life. As the final words of the book have it, in the end he dies "old and satisfied with days."

I began this chapter intending to reflect only on the divine speeches and ended by reflecting on chs. 38–42 as a whole. In doing this, I run the risk of ignoring the judgment of many recent interpreters that the epilogue offers a Hollywood ending that spoils the book's realism and worse still, that it reinstates the theology of reward that the book had spent so much energy refuting. Those interpreters typically conclude that therefore this ending must have been tacked on later by an obtuse, pious editor.

A young Jewish man was the only person in his family to survive the death camps. After the war he came to America and eventually met another survivor of the camps, a young Jewish women. They married and raised a family. In his free hours he became a volunteer coach to a high school soccer team. When asked, he would speak about his experiences to students in the school's modern history class. Dare anyone speak of his life as enjoying a Hollywood ending? Dare anyone suggest to him that those who died, including his own family, were less deserving of life than he? If anything, his life poses as much of a riddle for human understanding as the deaths of his family. But those who knew this man spoke of his kindness, his love for young people. To know the story of this man is to be in a position to read the epilogue in a new way. If, despite all that has happened, life can resume itself and go on, and even, now and then, give rise to singing, it is to be embraced, though from now on life is even more unfathomable than Job and his friends could previously have imagined.

8. Further on Job and Naomi

In Chapter Five I briefly compared the story of Job with the story of Naomi. In the present chapter I would like to return to that comparison, highlighting certain prominent similarities and then one striking, if implicit, contrast.

Before I begin this exploration, I want to suggest that, for all the prominence Ruth has in the book named after her, Ruth in fact plays a supporting role in a story that begins and ends with Naomi and is thereby really a story about her. The story opens on a family scene involving a man by the name of Elimelech and his wife, Naomi, who have two sons, Mahlon and Chilion. So far so good. But then a famine arises in the land. As our word "famished" indicates, famine is a state of chronic hunger. In that region, as the Elijah story of 1 Kings 17–18 illustrates, famine is typically a result of drought, when the earth is unable to produce vegetation for livestock and grain for people. So, like Abram and Sarai in Genesis 12, this family seeks to ride out the famine by going to another country. But Elimelech dies there, and then, after Mahlon and Chilion marry, but before they have any children, they too die, "so that the woman was bereft of her two sons and her husband" (Ruth 1:5) To be sure, Orpah and Ruth are also bereft. But this is not their story; it is Naomi's, so the narrative focus falls on her plight, which has two dimensions that she will shortly identify.

One day Naomi hears that in her home country "the Lord had visited his people and given them food" (Ruth 1:6). As in the Elijah story, the drought must have ended with returning rains, and the famine is about to end with an abundant barley harvest (Ruth 1:22). Encouraged by this news, Naomi sets off for her homeland with her two daughters-in-law. But on the way, she turns and urges them to return to the home of their respective mothers. (Why not their paternal home? Because this is a story centered in women?) She invokes the *hesed,* the kinship-kindness, of her God upon them for the kindness they have shown her and her sons. After some resistance, Orpah follows her urging and returns home, but Ruth, in words that have immortalized her loyalty, insists on casting her lot with Naomi and Naomi's God.

When Naomi and Ruth arrive home, the women's "Is this Naomi?" calls to mind the way Job's friends at first "did not recognize him" (Job 2:12). Their question provokes a response in which Naomi names her twofold plight. It is bad enough that, as she says, "I went away full, and the Lord has brought me back empty" (Ruth 1:21). Her plight is intensified by what she takes to be its religious significance. According to RSV and NIV, she says, "the Lord has afflicted me," and NRSV translates this, "the Lord has dealt harshly with me." But these renderings reflect the earliest translations of the Bible, the Greek and the Syriac, which take the Hebrew consonantal text *'nh* to indicate the verb *'innâ,* "afflict." In the Hebrew Bible, this consonantal text is provided with vowels that indicate the verb *'ānâ,* which in the present context means "testify against," and that is how the verse is translated in KJV as well as the marginal notes to RSV, NRSV, and NIV. I favor the KJV translation, as indicating that Naomi takes her calamity as a sign that God is for some reason displeased with her conduct and is testifying against her in and through what has happened to her. This, of course, is exactly how Job and his friends view Job's calamities. And, as in the case of Job, Naomi finds herself embittered, both over her bereavement and over what she takes to be God's unjust action against her. Her bitterness is intensified on account of her daughters-in-law, for now they have no husbands and she has no further sons to perform the duty of next of kin on behalf of the deceased.

At this point I will leap over the intervening narrative and move on to its resolution, which turns on the role of the next of kin. The next of kin, in this function, is termed a *gō'ēl,* or "redeemer." The *gō'ēl* in Israel was a near kin who, acting in a spirit of clan loyalty, performed the following sorts of acts on behalf of a clan member in need of help: (a) to take a widow to wife in order to raise up children bearing the name of her deceased husband; (b) to ransom a clan member from bondage due to debt; or to buy back a clan member's field forfeited for debt; and (c) to avenge a clan member's death. This function then was applied to God as a metaphor for God's action as Israel's "divine kinsman." As we have already seen, Job in 19:25 reaches out for such a figure to act on his behalf in his plight. In the book of Ruth, God will act as divine redeemer through the figure of Boaz, and I will return to that part of the narrative below. For now, I will move on to its resolution in ch. 4.

The first scene of the resolution takes place in the city gate (Ruth 4:1) where the male elders meet to transact the community's affairs. The action to be taken there has as its ultimate goal "to restore the name of the dead to his inheritance" (4:5, 10), by a son who would take his place among those male elders sitting in the gate (4:10). The male focus at this point in the story is not surprising, given the point of view and the concerns of all who are gathered in that gate. But this point of view and this concern then give way to the chief concern and point of view of the narrator, which, as is clear from 1:5, has to do with the figure of Naomi. So, with the birth of a son to Ruth and Boaz, the scene shifts from the male-centered gate to the circle of women first encountered in 1:19. In their eyes, Boaz functions as *gō'ēl*, not on behalf of the dead husband of Ruth, but on behalf of Naomi (4:14). As for the son, he will be significant, not for bearing the name of his deceased male ancestor, but for the way he will be to Naomi "a restorer of life and a nourisher of your old age" (4:15). And, when Naomi takes the infant to her breast and nurses him (4:16), the women name him "Obed," a name signifying for them that "a son has been born to Naomi" (4:17). How does "Obed" — a name formed from the masculine singular active participle of the verb *'ābad* and meaning "worker, servant" — in the present context connote "sonship"? Or, to put the question the other way around, in what sense does a son serve a parent? In the ancient world children served their parents' old age as their "social security," providing economic support and other care for them and in this way respecting them. (This is what the commandment means when it says, "Honor your father and your mother.") This "serving" aspect of the son-father relation is reflected in Mal 3:17: "a man spares his son who serves ['ōbēd] him." These women name the child (whom they speak of as "born to Naomi") Obed, for he is the one who will care for her in her old age (Ruth 4:15). If the men in the gate assume that he will bear the name of his male ancestors, the women enshrine in his name the significance his life has for his female ancestor Naomi.

In their beginnings and in their endings, then, the book about Job and the book about Naomi have much in common. But there is all the difference in the world between the two books in regard to what occurs between their respective beginnings and endings. It is, perhaps, the difference between the world of most men and the world of most women. One could have imagined that when Naomi spoke of God testifying against her, this would trigger a theological discussion between her and the women. Would they have begun (like Eliphaz) with encouragement, but then, in the face of her bitter protests against God, turned to accusation? Or if Naomi, exploiting the courtroom imagery implicit in her word "testified," sought a formal hearing before God, would they have served as witnesses on her behalf? The story does not address these narrative possibilities. Following Naomi's legal allusion, the closest the story comes to a courtroom denouement is the scene in the gate where the men of the city adjudicate the case Boaz puts before them. And here the issue is only a matter of who will perform the *gōʾēl* function. The whole concern, from beginning to end of Naomi's story, is how to deal with calamity in such a way as to restore those whose lives have been so grievously diminished. What a contrast with the almost interminable theological disputation in Job 3–26!

[margin: redeemer]

One could, then, take the book of Ruth and the book of Job as case studies in how to, and how not to, come to the aid of friends and neighbors who have suffered one or another of life's calamities. The besetting temptation of religious folk — especially those who are concerned with right doctrine — is to offer an explanation of why the calamity has happened and what God is doing in it. (I write this paragraph on the very day on which the *New York Times* carries a news item reporting how a pastor in Kansas views the death of several Amish schoolgirls at the hand of a gunman driven by self-hate and hatred of God.[1] Alluding to the gunman's confessed preoccupation with sexual molestation, the pastor's daughter is reported as saying, on a syndicated talk-radio program, "What [God] did with one stroke on that day, sending a pervert in — because America is a nation of perverts — it's appropriate he sent a pervert in to shoot those children. The Amish people were laid open to shame because they are a false religion." Such are the lengths to which religion can drive some folk.) The men and the women in the book of Ruth engage in no theological explanations. They just set about helping Naomi and her daughter-in-law get back on their feet. In this way they are the counterpart of Job's brothers, sisters, and kinfolk in Job 42:11. And, as I have suggested, if these groups in

---

1. *New York Times,* 6 October 2006, A14.

either community need explicit articulation of the theology they embody, it is provided in the divine speeches of Job 38–41.

In such a comparison, is the religious wrangling in Job 3–26 shown up as simply an exercise in intellectualizing futility? In light of the book of Ruth and the example of Job's family and acquaintances, it would be easy to draw such a conclusion. And that would be unfortunate. All of us come into life equipped in some measure with three ways of "comprehending" life's challenges: our hands, our heads, and our hearts. Some are especially good with their hands. They are the doers, who get things done. Without them, mourners would go hungry and people deprived of their homes by natural disasters would remain destitute. Some may be all thumbs, or have not the means, when it comes to practical help; but their hearts are as wide and deep as the ocean, and the moral support they offer, the comforting bosom for the aching heart, gives essential help. Then there are those whose gifts are gifts of the head, enabling the community as a whole to benefit from discoveries that make life easier, the earth more fruitful, and so on. Moreover, the drive to understand operates in us all; and those who excel in gifts of intellectual exploration, analysis, and interpretation benefit the whole community in their own way. But that very drive to understand can carry even its most gifted practitioners into depths where it is easy to fall into errors of analysis, errors of interpretation, errors of philosophical and doctrinal system-building. And the results of such intellectual labors, disseminated through the community as common sense, can also, through long familiarity, lose their sensitivity and freshness and become reduced to clichés and formulas that lose touch with the deeper mysteries of existence. What saves a person, a community, that has fallen into such errors, or become satisfied with such formulas, except the inbreaking of a reality that is more complex, more mysterious than those formulas to which those systems testify? When that happens, the questioning of long-held understandings of the world can feel like the loss of reality itself; the questioning of long-held understandings of God can feel like the absence or the death of God. In this respect, part of the grieving process — part of one's grief-work — consists in the sort of travail that Job and his friends go through between ch. 2 and ch. 42. There are those for whom the grief-work following a calamity is primarily economic and emotional, a matter of coming to terms with the pain of loss and the bleakness of life after that loss. But where there has been a deep investment in structures of religious understanding and those structures have been torn apart by calamity, the task of dropping one's understandings "in the middle of the road" and trying to "stack them in a better load" can be a long and painful intellectual travail that must be seen through until the questions at its heart are resolved or dissolved in a healing vision.

So I propose that the book of Ruth and the book of Job offer two kinds of scenarios for how a person and a community can move through a calamity in such a way as to recover an appetite for life. Neither approach need be played off against the other. If one may put the issue in terms of the biblical refrain, "How long, O Lord?" these two stories join in saying, "as long as it takes."

And what of those life stories that do not arrive at an ending like that of Job and Naomi but simply come to a dead end? Granted that the book of Job and the book of Ruth are about the stories of Job and Naomi and the others in those stories play supporting roles, what about Elimelech, and Mahlon and Chilion, and the children of Job? What to make of their stories? Or what to make of the stories of, for example, veterans of the Vietnam War with wounds that leave neurological damage whose legacy is unending pain and who, on hearing, day after day, of casualities to American troops in a more recent war, relive their own traumas until they come to the point where they can no longer bear the weight of it all and end their own lives? Is such an act simply a sitting down in the middle of the road and giving up there? Or may it also be an act of committing oneself, in mingled despair and hope, into those hands and that heart that alone can comprehend all extremes? During the exile, the prophet of the exile hears God say to Zion, "I have graven you on the palms of my hands" (Isa 49:16). It is in reliance on such a word that the psalmist says, "My times are in thy hand" and "into thy hand I commit my spirit" (Ps 31:15, 5). For it is the reliability of such a word, coming in Scripture, or heard in the kindness of others, or experienced in the renewal of the earth, coming as the scent of water to a thirsty soul, that is the ground of our hopes.

A Personal Epilogue in Three Parts

After all my work in the book of Job over a stretch of fifty-odd years, in the classroom, with evening groups in churches, and at my desk writing, this book continues to amaze me in its capacity to continue to speak a fresh "word in season." The following personal reports are offered to show what I mean, and also for their own commentary on this inexhaustible book. In offering these personal reports, I do not consider them privileged, immune from questioning or challenge. They are not offered as interpretive arguments, and certainly not as indicating how others should appropriate this book's meaning for their lives. They are offered simply as one person's testimony.

"Here am I"

It was the morning of November 9th, 2006. Earlier that Fall I had received word from Eerdmans that my manuscript on the book of Job, entitled "At the Scent of Water," had been favorably reviewed and was a candidate for publication. So I had turned my attention to another writing project, and on that morning was immersed in the book of Ecclesiastes, working on the verse in 4:6, which one scholar translates, "Better is one handful with quietness than two fists full with toil and a striving after wind." At 9:10 A.M. the phone rang. It was my urologist, with news that the prostate biopsy had come back positive. "But it's bizarre," he said. "I've had five different pathologists check it out, and they all agree." I had primary-site transitional cell carcinoma (TCC) of the prostate, an exceedingly rare, aggressive form of prostate cancer. He had to be out of town for over a week, so he scheduled November 22nd for a CT-scan and a consultation for us to consider the results.

The intervening thirteen days were unlike any I had ever spent. Oddly, I was not anxious. But suddenly I found myself in a strange space. All around me people were going on with their lives, their attitudes, their words, and their actions appearing to connect them in an unbroken stream with their past and their future. But my past and my future seemed to lie on the other side of a clear but impenetrable wall of glass, and inside that wall I existed in a moment-by-moment present that had no past and no future and that was only as wide as the distance between me and just short of the next person. I had often heard people counsel to "live in the moment." Was this what they meant?

I stopped work on Ecclesiastes. I searched through my shelves until I found a book that I had read years ago, Pierre Teilhard de Chardin's *The Divine Milieu*.[1] It was clear from my underlinings and marginal comments that I had read it carefully. Its basic thesis had stuck in my mind over the years. But then I had read it, I confess, with professional interest as a biblical exegete and amateur Christian theologian. Now I read it (as my wife Eileen says she reads Scripture) "as one going to the gallows." I ingested every page with a sense of the immediate relevance to me of its immense vision of Christian vocation in an evolutionary universe orchestrated by God as its Alpha and Omega. Teilhard's robust vision of human life as one of activity and creative achievement appealed to me, giving contemporary expression to the ancient saying of Irenaeus that (in his words) "the Glory of God is man alive" (*Against Heresies* 4.20.7). This vision Teilhard set out in a chapter which he called "The Divinisation of Our Activities." But it was the next chapter that especially spoke to me and helped me to enter into my condition in a centering and positive way. That chapter he called "The Divinisation of Our Passivities."

On the morning of November 22nd, Eileen and I walked along the long corridor from radiology to the urologist's office. I carried under my arm the huge manila envelope full of photographic plates, feeling like an emcee at Oscar night holding the envelope with the name of the next Oscar winner but not knowing yet what name it contained. Was my fate al-

1. Pierre Teilhard de Chardin, *The Divine Milieu: An Essay on the Interior Life* (New York: Harper, 1960).

ready sealed? But then the urologist went over the plates with us and showed us that there was no sign of any cancer outside the prostate. With a routine prostatectomy I should be in the clear.

A month later, I prepared to enter hospital for final tests and surgery the next morning. The intervening month had been filled with further reading in the vein of Teilhard. It had been a time rich in reflection and intense in its focus on what is most important in life. What, out of all this, would I take with me into the OR as my own last-minute "prep"? A golfing duffer, I had watched many instructional films that showed how a golfer can break down his swing into its component parts, practice each part, and then reassemble those parts into a coherent swing. And I had practiced such a process as best I could. But I also knew, from listening to the pros, that when standing over one's ball on the golf course, one should forget all those many individual learnings and, at most, have in one's mind only one "swing thought." "Keep your head down." Or "shift your weight." Or "straight left arm." What single "swing thought" might I take into the OR the next morning? I pondered this question for a while.

Suddenly it hit me. Job, ch. 38. What is the realization that comes to him in that chapter? Is it not a scene of all nature coming to life at the creative call of God? And is it not this scene that somehow moves Job to a new perspective, that implicitly invites him to become part of that picture again? Earlier, in working on the manuscript for this book, I had come to the conviction that the repeated references to rain in this chapter were part of God's answer to Job, responding to his words in 14:7-9. Suddenly, a phrase leapt out at me from the end of 38:34-35:

> Can you lift up your voice to the clouds,
> that a flood of waters may cover you?
> Can you send forth lightnings, that they may go
> and say to you, *hinnēnû* — "Here we are"?

Yes! When God calls the elements and the natural forces of the world into existence, they respond by saying, not in words (Ps 19:1-4), but in their very "standing forth" (as in Isa 48:13), *hinnēnû* — "Here we are." There it is! That's my swing thought!

To put it into context, I searched the Bible for other passages with this phrase. I found Gen 22:1, where God calls to Abraham and Abraham says, *hinnēnî* — "Here am I," and again Gen 22:7, where Isaac calls to his father and Abraham says, *hinnēnî* — "Here am I," and then again Gen 22:11, where the angel of the Lord calls to Abraham and he says, *hinnēnî* — "Here am I." I found 1 Sam 3:4-8, where three times Samuel repeats this phrase, thinking it is Eli who calls, and the fourth time, realizing that it is God who is calling him, says to God, *hinnēnî* — "Here am I." I found Isa 6:8, where God asks, "Whom shall I send, and who will go for me?" and Isaiah answers *hinnēnî* — "Here am I." And, discovering that the Greek translation of these passages reads *idou egō* — literally, "behold, I," I searched the Greek New Testament where I found Mary saying to the angel in Luke 1:38, *idou hē doulē kyriou* — "Behold the handmaiden of the Lord." And I recalled that one of the central themes in the Christian existentialist philosophy of Gabriel Marcel is what he calls *disponibilité,* by which I understand him to mean that to fully exist (as Irenaeus would put it, to be "fully alive") is to be fully present to the world around oneself in a spirit of availability and constructive interaction.

There's my swing thought! "Here am I." *hinnēnî.* In the OR, the medical personnel would be bringing all of their training, experience, dedication, and early-morning energy and making it available (*hinnēnû* — "Here we are"). The very OR equipment and surgical instruments; the blood that I had given earlier at the blood bank and now was ready for infusion as needed; the anesthetic — all these, in spirit or in matter, available to me. And my part in this? Well, I couldn't very well say to the OR personnel, *hinnēnî,* or even, "Here am I." But, like the voiceless creation, I could at least place my embodied self at their disposal in a spirit of availability and self-entrusting.

The next morning they wheeled me down the corridor, up the elevator to the fourth floor and down another serpentine corridor. When we reached the double doors to the OR the anesthesiologist said, "OK, you can get up and walk in." (I was, after all, in good physical condition.) I walked in through the doors and saw the operating table ringed with a group of what looked like twenty-somethings in greenish-blue gowns. I think it was their youth — as though they had not too long ago waited on tables — that moved me to walk up to this table, spread my hands out sideways in a gesture of self-presentation, and say, in my best wait-person personification, "Hi! My name is Gerry, and I'll be your patient this morning." I forget exactly how they responded (the anaesthetic does tend to erase OR memories); but my impression is that they caught my humor, answered in kind, and in short order (again, that erasure of memory thing) I found myself in recovery.

As it turned out, the CT-scan had been unable to pick up a large, diseased lymph node tucked underneath a cluster of dense tissues of various kinds. (When the surgeon described this scene, my lay imagination pictured an interwoven cluster of electrical wires and TV cables overlaying and hiding a golf ball.) After quick consultation, the medical team removed the diseased node along with its companions in that area, but left my prostate in place so that I could recover more quickly from the surgery so as to get on with regimens of chemotherapy and radiation.

The first regimen stretched over seventeen weeks of the most aggressive chemotherapy ("harshest, most toxic," in the oncologist's words), a regimen at times grueling, and at all times taking up all of my attention and energy simply to live "in the moment." Living in the moment, then, was no virtue, or spiritual practice. It was a necessity. Because throughout this time the end of this regimen was too far away for hope to reach; the thought of it only aroused an impatience that added to the burden of the present. The second regimen stretched over eight weeks of daily radiation. Throughout both regimens, administered by personnel for whom I have the greatest admiration and gratitude, my daily swing thought remained *hinnēnî,* "Here am I." It was my way of presenting myself for participation in a world much larger than myself. And it was my way of connecting personally with the Job whom I had observed and overheard so many times through all the years of teaching a "Job course." Often, in those courses, we would discover that someone in the class was going through, or had just gone through, a Joban experience. At such times I had felt that those persons were in a much better position than I to interpret this book, and I learned more than I can say from them. It is probably true to say that what they taught me, by their example as well as their words — their resilient willingness to enter into their experience and live in it and through it — came home to me and informed me at some deep level below consciousness, on that day when I discovered my swing thought in Job 38.

[I am not, in general, a journalkeeper. But for a variety of reasons, I decided to keep a log during the course of my treatments. Recently, in reading through a manuscript commentary on Job for a scholarly acquaintance, something he wrote on the divine speeches led me to reread one of the entries in my log. I reproduce that entry here for its thematic connection to the above account.

Monday, May 7, 2007. 9:30 A.M. I've been sitting in the recliner thinking up a thick vegetable soup for drinking its broth. It's maybe 58°F out-side, but the sun is bright, the air clear, and all the colors are sharp. A mo-ment ago the maple tree was dancing in the breeze, as though "for sheer morning gladness" (Robert Frost), purely for its own sake, with no thought of me. How *could* it think of me. That's not its business.

There! Now the tree is just bobbing and bowing gently. I think what is so beautiful about the tree is the inutility of its being there. It is being *itself* (like the little girl and the three boys at the Cummings the other evening — obliv-ious to all that was around them, so caught up were they in their respective worlds of play). It is its lack of concern for me, its utter selfness — just its *hinnēnî*, "Here I am" — that I find so *engaging*, so *encouraging*. I am so *grate-ful*, that in the midst of this chemotherapy — where every need to eat, to drink fluids, is a distasteful effort, and my weakness defeats any possibility of *doing* anything except what will babysit my mind; and it is too risky to think of what the outcome of the chemotherapy will be, or the following course of treatment — all that has to be left in limbo — in the midst of all this, I am so *grateful* for that tree — its objective otherness, doing me no good, asking nothing of me, just once again, after its winter of bareness, now dancing in its leafy greenness, oblivious to the trees uprooted and blown down by the horrific tornado in Kansas a few days ago. Is this something like the aware-ness that comes over Job in chs. 38-39 and then, more so, in 40-41?

It is remarkable that Freud and I can experience this otherness/indiffer-ence of nature so differently. Put the question more broadly, in re: the de-bate whether nature in any way intimates the existence and presence of a Creator. It may all turn on the assertorial freight we are willing to recognize in the "nevertheless" in Frost's poem "The Tuft of Flowers."[2] Are human na-ture and nonhuman nature "too widely met" (like the parties in Frost's "A Missive Missile") for us to have any idea whether we are misreading nature, or reading into it? The very attempt to settle the question scientifically seems doomed from the outset. I recline here and notice how the breeze striking the sweet gum and the maple at different times gives them the ap-pearance of dancing and talking with each other. And my heart, my spirit, moves within me, and the movement is one of appreciation and gratitude. And the gratitude is not for what this scene does for *me;* it is for what the scene is for and in itself.

And I am grateful to God for the *gratuity* of the scene — its utter inutility.

2. *Collected Poems, Prose, & Plays* (New York: Library of America, 1995) 31.

Rain to Satisfy the Waste and Desolate Land

It was a Sunday morning during the Advent season of 2006. I was sitting in a pew, at the early service, alongside a longtime friend whom I shall call Jean. As usual, she wore her portable oxygen cannister suspended from her shoulder strap. Cancer had necessitated removal of one lung years ago, she suffered emphysema in the other lung, and during the previous week she herself had undergone a biopsy. I leaned over and asked how the biopsy had turned out. She turned to me, put her hand gently on my forearm and, with the look in her eye that I had come to treasure for its resilient good spirits, smiled as she said, "Gerry, this will be my last Advent." She had declined the recommendation of a regimen of treatment, knowing that at her age the slight prolongation of her life that it could at best offer would not compensate for its rigors.

A week or two later I underwent my surgery. One would suppose that the last face a person recovering from cancer surgery would wish to see at the foot of one's hospital bed would be that of someone dying of cancer. But outside of my own family, it was Jean who then, and in subsequent months through regular phone calls, did the most to cheer me up and encourage me along my path. Later, when I was able to call on her and her husband at their retirement apartment, thinking to offer her some return for her many kindnesses to me, I invariably came away knowing that I had once again been the one ministered to. Her good humor and her honesty in the face of her approaching death were infectious.

Despite her prediction, she did live through another Advent. At the end of my last visit with them, on the last Saturday in the year, her husband accompanied me to the door and mentioned that Jean hoped I would give the homily at her service. Inwardly I quailed at the thought, but I said, "Yes, that would be an honor."

I quailed, because for me preaching is an impossibility. I am not known for my hesitation in speaking. I am an all-too-verbose person. All too often I had run over the bell signaling the end of a class period. But a homily, a sermon, is not the place for venting one's pet ideas or exploring aloud with others one's favorite heuristic questions. The challenge of speaking in the pulpit in such a way as, just perhaps, to have the sow's ear of one's own words become, by the grace of God and the working of the Spirit, a silk purse containing God's Word to others is a challenge that I have consistently confronted as an impossibility, my personal experience of the truth of Jesus' saying that "With humans this is impossible, but with God all things are possible." So it was that, in due course, I gave a homily on one of the passages that Jean's husband, a lay reader in the church, had chosen to be read. My theme was "Treasure in an Earthen Vessel." By the grace of God I was enabled to weave Jean's life and witness in with an exposition of 2 Cor 4:6–5:9 in such a way that that passage interpreted her life and her dying, even as (as one person said) her life and her dying opened up the meaning of that passage in a fresh way.

Later I reflected on the experience I once again had in preparing that homily: an initial feeling of inadequacy, followed by a preliminary resort to conventional clichés and at the same time an awareness of how stale they would sound; yet, an inner resistance to the effort it would take to move beyond the familiar, an inner resistance to the need to move beyond what I already "knew" and into a kind of no-man's-land where I must be content to dwell for who knows how long until an appropriate idea — or rather, an appropriate seed image — would emerge and a homily, by fits and starts, would begin to take shape. I had often pictured that period of thematic disorientation as a no-man's-land. But suddenly, as that image came to me again and I tried to put that experience into words for myself, I found myself recurring once again to Job ch. 38 and another of its passages about the life-giving rain (38:25-27).

> Who has cleft a channel for the torrents of rain,
> and a way for the thunderbolt,
> to bring rain on a land where no man is,
> on the desert in which there is no man;
> to satisfy the waste and desolate land,
> and to make the ground put forth grass?

I had long pondered this passage, which appears to celebrate God's concern to "satisfy" (the Hebrew word means, literally, to "sate" an appetite) an uninhabited region for its own sake. And I had taken it as one means whereby God in these chapters seeks to draw Job beyond his own anthropocentric concerns and to reintroduce him to a wider world charged with the dynamism of a created life worthwhile beyond any consideration of its utility to human enterprise. But this time, on an impulse, I decided to examine the terms in the last four lines: "land," "desert," "waste and desolate land," and "ground." What I discovered once again presented the message of the book of Job to me in a fresh way, this time helping me finally to gain a perspective on my decades-long experience of the impossible task of preaching.

The first word is, in Hebrew, *'ereṣ*, the most generic term for "earth." The second word is *midbār*, which is a specific sort of "earth" — a wilderness, of the sort described, for example, in Jer 2:6 as "a land of deserts and pits, a land of drought and deep darkness, a land that none passes through, where no man dwells." But the following two words in Hebrew, *šō'â* and *měšō'â*, describe that wilderness in a very specific way. Coming from the same verbal root, they refer in one way or another to a "devastation or ruin," of a city such as Babylon (Isa 10:3; 47:11), or of a temple (Ps 74:3), or, figuratively, of a human life (Ps 73:18). In each case these words refer, literally or figuratively, to a place that had once been cultivated, built up, given humanly meaningful form and order, and inhabited as something familiar and understood, but now, through some terrific force, has been thrown into ruins and rendered desolate, humanly abandoned, left to return to a state of nature. So Job apparently felt about his life. For in 30:14 he had described himself with the image of a city under attack by those who had breached its walls and rolled on amid the "crash" *(šō'â)* of its walls and buildings. The result was to leave him abandoned in a wilderness inhabited only by wild creatures such as jackals and ostriches (30:29-31).

But it is precisely to such a region that God's rain comes. To what purpose? The NRSV reads, in 38:27, "to make the ground put forth grass." But the Hebrew word behind "ground" is, again, a very specific term: *mōṣā'* — "source, place of coming forth, place of producing." God's rain comes in order to turn that dry, drought-stricken wilderness (as in Jer 2:6) into a source of lush vegetation, food for all the wild grazing animals and birds that roam within it (Job 39:1-18).

It is when Job has entered deeply into the wilderness of his experience, in a no-man's-land devoid of the marks of human habitation, human meaning-making, that Job finds the rain for which he, as a felled tree, had earlier (in ch. 14) expressed a wistful longing. And in a much smaller way, I realized, it is when I have been willing to abandon my favorite familiar clichés of interpretation and understanding and let them fall, as it were, into ruin, willing to move past my resistance to the void where all meaning is as yet inchoate and unfamiliar — it is then that, to the extent that it does happen, I have found the grace of God's rain to turn this barren and drought-stricken human servant, against all odds, into a source, or rather a medium, of a word that others may find helpful and life-encouraging.

As I entered the regimen of chemotherapy, a fellow retired priest of the church who was also entering treatment for a second onset of cancer wrote to encourage me as, in his words, I was now entering strange territory and would be learning to walk without the aid of familiar landmarks. The experience of those regimens, and in its own way my repeated experience over the decades in preparing to give a sermon or homily, are only two forms of what I have come to recognize as a disciples' path that so many walk on in so many different specific ways. It involves a willingness to move, or a being thrown by circumstances, into the unfamiliar and the threatening, where the grace of God, when it comes, is recognized as a grace that had come formerly through familiar channels but now comes with all the freshness of that first day of creation when "the morning stars sang together, and all the children of God shouted for joy" (Job 38:7).

Job and My Parents

Finally, I want to offer a testimony that is not mine but that of my parents. It comes through a letter that my mother wrote to my father in 1936, on the back of which he had written a series of thoughts evoked by his circumstances and by her letter. This document has a back-story that I may summarize in the following way.

Our parents were of Mennonite stock. Their ancestors had fled religious persecution in the Netherlands, migrating with other Mennonites to Danzig (now Gdansk) in what was then part of Prussia, and from there to Russia in the time of Catherine the Great. An initial period of hospitality, or at least tolerance, eventually turned to hostility, and another migration took many Mennonites to Western Canada. Our father was born in Russia and came over with his parents at the age of six months; our mother was born in Canada shortly after her parents arrived. In due course her father became a prosperous miller, and she one of almost a dozen siblings all of whom played musical instruments and tennis. She loved school, especially mathematics, and cried for weeks when her father informed her after grade six that his daughters would never have to work for a living so she could discontinue school now and come home to perfect her domestic and musical arts. Our father initially followed his father's footsteps as a tinsmith and "minored" also as a carpenter. (I have his "monkey wrench" on a shelf over my computer as I write; our daughter, who has inherited his carpentering skills, has his toolbox, expertly made from heavy sheet tin and strip iron.) But in his teens he was exposed, in an unforeseen circumstance, to prolonged cold weather, and a bout with rheumatic fever damaged his heart. A naturally robust physique began to break down, and by the time I knew him he was unable to work steadily — a furnace for this neighbor; a breadbox for that neighbor; a summer spent making doormats out of old tires, with drills and riggings fashioned from discarded farm machinery; some blueberry pickers made from tin syrup pails and steel knitting needles, expertly soldered and, after sixty years of use, still in pristine condition (each of us four brothers has one, bought back recently from farmers who had used them until retirement); but no steady work.

But our father's mind was as energetic as ever. Possessed of less formal education than our mother, he read voraciously, especially in the area of politics (he subscribed to *Hansard,* the official verbatim report of the daily debates in the Canadian House of Commons), and he wrote poetry. His political views were, shall we say, decidedly leftist; and from his caustic comments on the radio sermons that followed the Sunday morning reports from Parliament Hill, I gathered that he thought religion so much "pie in the sky," and the established churches lackeys of the political and economic establishment. His intellectual energies also moved him to participate vigorously in local expressions of countercultural political movements, and many were the afternoons and evenings when I sat in a corner and listened, my imagination stretched to the corners of the earth, while he and his local cronies hosted provincial and national leaders of these movements — and indeed, one person who had succeeded in being elected to the House of Commons — as they talked of international tariffs, workers' movements in other countries, and the inevitable inequities and injustices of free enterprise capitalism. But his physical health continued to deteriorate, and when I was thirteen and he forty-seven, he died.

His death plunged me into an existential funk that increased in intensity until a crisis in the autumn following graduation from high school and, a year later, a conversion experience that brought me to church and confirmation and then sent me to seminary. Our mother's brother and two of his sons were ordained clergy in the Church of the New Jerusalem (Swedenborgian); and she herself was a devout member of the New Church. I knew, then, that, though I did not follow her and her family denominationally, I had her full moral support. But I often wondered what our father would think of me. In the Anglican Church, of all places — in his eyes the chaplaincy of imperial England in Canada — would he see me as betraying all that he had come to stand for? Yet I knew that I had to respond to what claimed me as he had to what claimed him; and I could only hope he would at least respect that.

Fast forward to the year 2003. I am auditing a course at my seminary on "Affect in Human Transformation," along with our daughter who is in a degree program in Marriage and Family Therapy. As part of a class report on "nostalgia" as a fundamental affect in my own life, and its imperceptibly gradual transformation over the years from an earlier pathological intensity, I decide to illustrate a point by quoting from a sermon on loneliness that I had preached during my seminary days. I find the sermon in an old cardboard box in the basement, stored underneath the desk where in 1982 I had written my commentary on Job. But what I also find brings about a transformation in self- and family-understanding that is instantaneous and electrifying. I find a letter, which I immediately recognize as being from our mother to our father and in the same instant realize that I have somehow never seen before, a letter written to him on August 30, 1936 (when I was four years old), and on the back of her letter his penciled handwriting. The immediate setting of this letter is as follows.

Our father's inability to put in a full workday did give him a good deal of free time. His political convictions and the communitarian ethics inherited from his Mennonite forebears moved him to an intense interest in the plight of recent immigrants to our small town and the outlying farms, people who, like us, suffered from the economic woes of the early thirties. Since many of these immigrants came from eastern Europe and knew little or no English, he became something of a spokesperson and advocate for them in their petitions to the government officer who administered the local program of economic "relief." The time came when our father found it necessary to apply for relief on our own behalf, but by this time the officer and his office staff had become heartily sick of his frequent appearances for all and sundry; and as a result, whenever he called at the office the officer was never in. So one Saturday evening he made his way unsteadily on foot, aided by his cane, to the man's home, three or four blocks from our place. The man's car was parked outside, but initial knockings failed to bring him to the door. So our father rapped more loudly, using the head of his cane. Finally the man came to the door, opened it, and (no doubt tired from a busy week) told our father rather testily that he would see him in the office on Monday; whereupon, in a surge of irritation, he gave the

128

screen-door a push outward as if to sweep his unwelcome caller off the small step and onto the walk below. Out father, thrust backward, threw his arms forward to regain his balance, and in the process struck the corner of the screen door with his cane, knocking a chip off the corner of the wooden frame. Turning away, he walked home, resolving that on Monday he would hold the officer to his promise.

On Monday morning our father and my second oldest brother were about to begin working on a doormat in the lean-to at the back of our house, when the town constable appeared with a warrant for his arrest on a charge of attempted murder. Apparently, the other man had phoned the constable in a panic on Saturday evening and shouted into the mouthpiece, "John Janzen has just tried to kill me!"

The powers that be in this little town had for some time resented our father's political views and his social activism on behalf of "the little man," as he put it, and now they felt they had him. But as the trial day came around, it was realized that a charge of attempted murder was ridiculous and could not be made to stick. So they proposed to reduce the charge to attempted breaking and entry. Our father — acting as his own counsel — said he didn't care what they charged him with, since he hadn't done anything; but that was his mistake. In support of that charge there was the chip broken off the screen door, and his conviction was followed by a sentence of thirty days in the provincial penitentiary. One of my brothers remembers that he spent most of that time in the prison infirmary, too sick for work on the prison farm or time unattended in a cell. Eventually he was released with time off for good behavior. I remember from my preteen years the stories he would tell of the sort of life the inmates contrived within the constraints of the prison; and I remember from my late teens — after he died — coming across a Bible in his desk and, reading it in desperation in the throes of my above-mentioned existential crisis, noted his penciled remarks in the margins of some of its pages. That Bible (his Low German Mennonite heritage led him to spell it Bibel) has been lost; but the memory of those penciled remarks, and the sight of his penned remarks in our mother's German Bibel that I still have, comes vividly to mind in light of the letter I shall now reproduce.

Our mother wrote to him on the second day of his incarceration. His penciled comments begin on the back of the page, appearing to start an inch down from the top margin, with the words, "salm 27." On the third day after finding this letter, in the attempt to make out why one of the sentences just above a fold in the page seemed to break off without a concluding word (see the *), I held the page up close to the desk lamp. Suddenly I realized that he had written four lines with some sharp instrument — a pin perhaps — as though in such a fever to get his thoughts down that he could not wait to find a pencil — and that on the fifth line he had scratched a capital "P" before someone put a pencil into his hand. Here is what he wrote (the scratched lines are in lighter print):

We have cried from beneath the crushing load of burdens too heavy to be borne and anxieties too grinding to endure. We cried long and earnestly but no answer came, and we thought to have fainted beneath the added weight of the Lord's silence. Psalm 27. But somehow we endured; and looking back upon it all, we wonder at the reserve strength which we found within ourselves when the day was evil and our prayers went unheard. But our prayers <u>were</u> heard. God answered us by the coming of the noonday angel whose name is "strength of the day." The needed strength was not dropped upon us as a miracle from heaven; it is God's gracious and kindly way to give us his best gifts in so unobtrusive and interior fashion that they seem to be our own, part of our natural equipment. In the day when I cried, Thou answeredst me; we only knew that where we expected weakness, there we found strength.

"Oh! what a miscarriage" to be judged with the judgment of men. The man of mere book learning "the ass carrying a load of books," we admire the man who converses rapidly in seven languages, and ignore him who can "speak a word in season to him that is weary." We have many who can give us information, but few whose touch quickens the *

We lay the difficulties and problems of the day before God. We beseech his help and claim his unfailing care. Again and again we catch ourselves thinking more of our needs and desires than of His majesty and grace. Petition crowds praise into a narrow corner. Anxiety puts a drag on adoration. We clutch feverishly at the Saviour's garments instead of listening calmly to His voice.

(There is hardly a Christian worker who has not, at some time or another, been tempted to regard this or that individual as a mere means to an end – a useful asset in the promotion of a pet scheme or the maintenance of a cherished institution. What is this at bottom but to use that which is intrinsically precious in God's sight as a mere pawn in the game? Self interest need not be mercenary in order to be godless. It may take the form of devotion to a cause, but in essence it is nothing less than a subtle translation of the coarse and patent profanity of the Ephesian tradesman.)

130

"We may follow Job through the furnace of affliction." (We must first sanctify ourselves, before we can give bread to the poor in such a fashion as shall make the gift a blessing ~~instead~~ and not a curse.

The last lines come at the bottom of the back page of the letter. The front page contains the following comments, which display a shift in mood, as though the existential immediacy of the previous page had by now given way to a more quiet reflection. The comments are separated by a line, as indicated.

The Atheist: The thought comes like the humming bird to pierce the bark and drain the sap. He is like the bricklayer who doesn't give thought to the problem of ventilation nor lighting arrangements in the building yet would quit in disgust because the contractor did not explain the whole plan. who himself does not know the ultimate desire of fulfillment of the architect nor the part the building will take in the final scheme of the Landlord.

The Bibel, religion, culture. If we have not the <u>law</u> but try our best we are a law unto ourself. We ~~often~~ adapt the bibel to our own sentiments each one builds his own religion, but most of us get not outside recognition. The Bibel is a true story of people in the sands of time wherefrom we can take examples and profit thereby.

Sympathy is a poor substitute for charity This thing that we call civilization by reason of the assumption that we are apart and on a higher plane than the animal kingdom ~~however forces us to~~ and by the fact that we admit there is a God who radiates grace and charity and conceitedly believing ourself to be next to Godliness, we are prone to ~~switching~~ pawn sympathy as charity not perceiving that the former is but a mat to the door of the latter and that in that belief we deceive no one but ourselves.

What staggered me with a sense of joyous wonder was the biblical ring of all these sentences — a spirit and tone I had encountered so often in the Psalms, not to mention Job — and the intimate knowledge of Scripture they reflected. The way my Dad moved from explicit quotation to implicit allusion and thematic resonance with Scripture showed that in his deepest soul he was at home there. The exegete in me wants to draw attention to the following examples.

"We thought to have fainted" (Ps 27:13 KJV "I had fainted"); repeated references to "strength" (opening and closing verses of Psalm 27); "To be judged with the judgment of men" (Ps 27:12); "In the day when I cried" (Ps 138:3); "a word in season to him that is weary" (Isa 50:4 KJV; also in that context the theme of false accusation); "clutch feverishly at the Saviour's garments" (the woman in Matt 9:20 with an issue of blood); "listening calmly to his voice" (Mary at Jesus' feet in Luke 10:38-42); "The Ephesian tradesman" (Acts 19:24-28; note a vocational tie between this metalworker, albeit a silversmith, and my father as a tinsmith. The passage would have intrigued him for the way a person can corrupt and betray his craft and guild); "Through the furnace of affliction" (Isa 48:10). What amazes me about all this is the way my Dad's own thoughts segue in and out of Scripture without breaking rhetorical stride. Only someone whose imagination was saturated with Scripture could write like that.

The three paragraphs on the front of the letter have the feel of someone who has gradually, since the parenthetical paragraph, been moving away from the white heat of his present predicament and reflecting in a more unhurried, philosophical vein on life issues. The first paragraph resumes the perspective of a tradesman, in this instance a bricklayer. My father, as a tinsmith, had on one occasion worked to insert tin "flashing" around the base of a brick chimney that someone else had constructed for a house yet others — carpenters — had erected. He would have been personally acquainted with the difference between the individual craftsman, with his limited assignment, and the general vision and plan of a building.

The second paragraph echoes, of course, Rom 2:14. The third, expressing both our Dad's concern for social justice and his critique of the church as offering empty solace, connects in interesting ways with the earlier parenthetical paragraph, by its reuse of the word "pawn" with similar connotations. Finally, one may note the image of sympathy as "mat" to the door of "charity" and reflect on the fact that Dad received the summons with its charge of attempted murder while he and Otto were preparing for a morning's work making doormats!

In all of this, filial love moves me to discern a family resemblance between my father and myself, in the way our scriptural and natural imagination uses images to make our points. But what this letter brings home to me above all, in its Joban reference, is that while for so many decades I thought to have worked alone, unable to reach my father's thought in my scriptural studies, all along, though separated by the widest of chasms, we had in some manner been working together. In fact, this document had lain in that cardboard box, inches from my feet, unknown to me while I wrote the commentary on Job.

But who or what was the "noonday angel whose name is 'strength of the day' "? For the life of me I cannot connect that passage with anything in the Bible. But my Dad goes on to say that this "noonday" experience was not magical. In what I take to be the profoundest theological depth of this whole letter, he writes, "It is God's gracious and kindly way to give us his best gifts in so unobtrusive and interior fashion that they seem to be our own, part of our natural equipment." What was that "unobtrusive and interior fashion"?

Blueberries.

In summer, in berry season, our Dad would take us blueberry picking. In 1936 the trial and Dad's term in prison made that impossible. Lying in prison — whether in his cell or in the prison hospital — Dad was no doubt sick with worry over the family's well-being. (My mother was four months pregnant at the time with the little one who turned out to be the elder of my two young sisters.) Did the mail come at noon? Or did he reread the letter at noon? And did the sight of her handwriting, and her ordinary everyday narrative (no doubt designed to reassure him even if her own soul was disquieted, like the woman in Psalm 131, over "things too overwhelming and too difficult" for her), and the recollection of her sweet, stout comradeship through thick and thin suddenly arise within his own sense of weakness and fill him with strength? Was it this letter that spoke a word in season to him in his weariness, its touch quickening something in him?

And was it the blueberries they had in common that was the vehicle of the gracious, kindly, and unobtrusive presence and grace of the God who is giver of the blessings of heaven above and the earth beneath? This is her letter:

Aug. 30 1936

Dear John,

Well, two days have passed and by & by 30 days will have gone by and everything will be as usual again. You know I told you just before you left that Paul D. had promised the boys 8¢ for their berries. Well he got cold feet and had one excuse after another for not coming for them, so yesterday towards evening Martin & Joe went up town and got a buyer here from down south and he gave them 5¢. Martin said they were lucky to get that, for he'd seen some berries this man had that he paid 7¢ for and they were much bigger and nicer ones than these, and Joe's and Atley's were wet all through. If they had been as dry as Martin's they would have got a little more.

How are you getting along, getting enough to read? I've spent the day writing letters (with Martin's new fountain pen. (He paid 1.00). I wrote to Isaac & Jake, Dave, & Mr. Walther.

As far as I know nothing unusual has happened since you left. We'll do our best to keep everything in shape and you watch out for your health.

With love & kisses from
me & the Boys. Agnes.

Frost's poem "The Tuft of Flowers" tells of a farmhand sent into a field to turn grass that had been mowed by another hand earlier in the day. Feeling the solitude of his task, but thinking of his fellow worker who had finished mowing then "gone his way," the farmhand concludes that "I must be, as he had been, — alone." Then a butterfly draws his attention to a small flower that the mower had taken care to avoid. The tuft of flowers strikes him as "a message from the dawn," and, imagining that earlier scene, he suddenly is alone no longer:

> But glad with him, I worked as with his aid,
> And weary, sought at noon with him the shade;
>
> And dreaming, as it were, held brotherly speech
> With one whose thought I had not hoped to reach.
>
> 'Men work together,' I told him from the heart,
> 'Whether they work together or apart.'[3]

If our Dad's reflections are my "tuft of flowers," joining us across the years in following Job through his furnace of affliction, what served as his? What "unobtrusive," "natural" artifact may have been instrumental in his sudden discovery of strength where he only expected weakness? I cannot prove it; but I suspect it was our Mother's letter. She no doubt was worried sick over him. But the letter is simply a cheerfully matter-of-fact report on her oldest son Martin picking blueberries with cousin Joe and friend Atley,

3. *Collected Poems, Prose, & Plays,* 31.

and selling them for 5¢ a pound, and her now writing the letter with the pen he bought for a dollar, and otherwise assuring Dad things will be okay at home while he is away. Our Mother and our Dad were two people who enduringly knew how to work together, whether they worked together or apart. And, I now see, they learned to do that, each in their own way, from the God they knew through the faith they inherited from their Mennonite ancestors. For all our father's passion for social and economic justice, a passion that our mother shared with him, they both were grounded in a faith that finds its deepest nourishment in cultivation of the earth and finding in its fruitfulness — even to blueberries — the evidence of God's sustaining goodness.

Acknowledgments

The author and publisher gratefully acknowledge permission to include material from the following sources:

Diagrams (pp. 72-73 herein) and excerpts from INTERPERSONAL WORLD OF THE INFANT by DANIEL STERN Copyright © 1985 by Basic Books, Inc. Reprinted by permission of BASIC BOOKS, a member of Perseus Books Group.

Table (p. 70 herein) used with permission from *Life and Faith: Psychological Perspectives on Religious Experience* by W. W. Meissner, SJ (Washington, DC: Georgetown UP, 1987).

Robert Frost, "The Armful," from THE POETRY OF ROBERT FROST edited by Edward Connery Lathem. Copyright 1928, 1930, 1934, 1939, 1969 by Henry Holt and Company, copyright 1956, 1958, 1962 by Robert Frost, copyright 1967 by Lesley Frost Ballantine. Reprinted by arrangement with Henry Holt and Company, LLC.

Excerpt from Robert Frost, "The Tuft of Flowers," from THE POETRY OF ROBERT FROST edited by Edward Connery Lathem. Copyright 1928, 1930, 1934, 1939, 1969 by Henry Holt and Company, copyright 1956, 1958, 1962 by Robert Frost, copyright 1967 by Lesley Frost Ballantine. Reprinted by arrangement with Henry Holt and Company, LLC.

Excerpt from Robert Frost, "The Masque of Reason," from THE POETRY OF ROBERT FROST edited by Edward Connery Lathem. Copyright 1928, 1930, 1934, 1939, 1969 by Henry Holt and Company, copyright 1956, 1958,